Dashiell Hammett

RECOGNITIONS

detective/suspense
Bruce Cassiday, General Editor

Raymond Chandler by Jerry Speir
P. D. James by Norma Siebenheller
John D. MacDonald by David Geherin
Victorian Masters of Mystery: From Wilkie Collins to Conan Doyle
by Audrey Peterson
Ross Macdonald by Jerry Speir
The Murder Mystique: Crime Writers on Their Art
edited by Lucy Freeman
Roots of Detection: The Art of Deduction before Sherlock Holmes
edited by Bruce Cassiday
Dorothy L. Sayers by Dawson Gaillard
Sons of Sam Spade: The Private Eye Novel in the 70s
by David Geherin

science fiction/fantasy
Sharon Jarvis, General Editor

Fritz Leiber by Tom Staicar
Isaac Asimov by Jean Fiedler and Jim Mele
Ray Bradbury by Wayne L. Johnson
Critical Encounters: Writers and Themes in Science Fiction
edited by Dick Riley
Critical Encounters II: Writers and Themes in Science Fiction
edited by Tom Staicar
The Feminine Eye: Science Fiction and the Women Who Write It
edited by Tom Staicar
Frank Herbert by Timothy O'Reilly
Ursula K. LeGuin by Barbara J. Bucknall
Theodore Sturgeon by Lucy Menger

Dashiell Hammett

Dennis Dooley

Frederick Ungar Publishing Co.
New York

For Elizabeth

"The Thin Man." Copyright © 1967 by Donald Justice. Reprinted from *Night Light* by permission of Wesleyan University Press.

Lines from *The Divine Comedy* by Dante Alighieri. Translated by Lawrence Grant White. Translation copyright © 1948 by Pantheon Books, Inc. Reprinted by permission of the publisher.

Lines from *The Inferno* by Dante Alighieri. Translated by John Ciardi. Copyright © 1954, 1982 by John Ciardi. Reprinted by arrangement with New American Library.

Lines from "Hugh Selwyn Mauberley." Copyright © 1926 by Ezra Pound. Reprinted from *Personae* by permission of New Directions Publishing Corporation.

Library of Congress Cataloging in Publication Data

Dooley, Dennis.
Dashiell Hammett.

(Recognitions)
Bibliography: p. 165
Includes index.
1. Hammett, Dashiell, 1894-1961—Criticism and interpretation. 2. Hammett, Dashiell, 1894-1961—Characters—Sam Spade. 3. Detective and mystery stories, American—History and criticism. I. Title. II. Series.
PS3515.A4347Z62 1984   813'.52   84-139
ISBN 0-8044-2141-2
ISBN 0-8044-6124-4 (pbk.)

THE THIN MAN

I indulge myself
In rich refusals.
Nothing suffices.

I hone myself to
This edge. Asleep, I
Am a horizon.

—Donald Justice

Contents

	Acknowledgments	vii
	Clues to the Reader	ix
1	Hell's Pavement: The Unintended Era	1
2	A New Kind of Detective: Four Stories of 1924	19
3	The Poet of Violence: Pain and Detachment in Early Hammett	33
4	Crooks and Capitalists: The Idealist Goes Armed	45
5	A Moll Named Grace: The Search for Wholeness	59
6	The Evil That Men Do: *Red Harvest*	73
7	Dead Souls: *The Dain Curse*	87
8	The Wages of Commitment: *The Maltese Falcon* and *The Glass Key*	99
9	Time's Shadow: *The Thin Man*	117
10	The Murder of Innocence: Hammett's Place	133
	Notes	149
	Bibliography	165
	Index	171

Acknowledgments

I am indebted to many people, beginning with my great friend, the late Max Levey, another "thin man" given to "rich refusals," who endured similar sufferings at the hands of McCarthyism. To him I owe an appreciation for the depth of conviction and the anguish experienced by those who, like Hammett and himself, took the high road to personal ruin for their souls' sake—as well as an appreciation for how contradictory impulses of monumental scope can coexist in the same person.

To Tom and Peg Campbell, best of friends, I owe several months at Dogwood, which enabled me to write a large piece of this book in positively idyllic circumstances—sitting at my typewriter by a roaring fire, looking out of a picture window at an expanse of snow-covered woods and blessed stillness broken only by an occasional jackrabbit. (The rest was written in far more prosaic—and I suspect common—circumstances, at the diningroom table between ten at night, when the last child went to sleep, and two in the morning.)

I owe thanks, also, to my original editor, Dick Riley, on whose conscience this entire project must lie; and his successor, Bruce Cassiday, and Cynthia Payne, who guided this book to its completion with extreme patience and understanding. That said, I must own responsibility for any mistakes or missteps, large or small, which may have crept or been forcibly dragged into this book on my end. And, all these years later, I find I must acknowledge a debt to my professors at Loyola and Indiana universities, who taught me how to read, and to my mother, Avis McMullin Dooley, who showed me the human heart.

Finally, I owe more than I can say to my own children—Ben, Chris, Heather (whose doll house has lain unfinished in the back of the basement for many months), and Claire—for their cheerful indulgence throughout what must often have seemed an interminable process—but especially to my wife and best counselor, Elizabeth Berrey for her good humor, patience, wisdom, and, most of all, her faithfulness to her convictions.

I have tried hard to produce a book none of them would be ashamed to be associated with.

Clues to the Reader

The preeminence of Dashiell Hammett's position in the world of twentieth-century detective fiction and his influence on the genre are a matter of more or less common consent: propositions that have attained the status of received truths. But when one considers the incredibly brief span of Hammett's career as a productive author, his stature as a writer becomes cause for astonishment. The five novels on which his reputation are based—*Red Harvest, The Dain Curse, The Maltese Falcon, The Glass Key,* and *The Thin Man*— were all published between 1929 and 1934, a period of barely five years.

The fact that Hammett published virtually nothing of any significance in the remaining two-and-a-half decades of his life has only deepened the fascination of latter-day Americans with this enigmatic figure.

More than fifty years after they first appeared in print, Hammett's novels and stories, later collected into book form, still captivate readers with the authority of their craft, the credible characters and wonderfully drawn action scenes, the canny air of authenticity with which they capture the mood and texture of the twenties underworld and the work of real detectives, and Hammett's own special blend of a sometimes chilling cynicism and a deeply rooted sense of honor. But, to be entirely honest, time has also taken a certain toll.

One hears from friends sent off to read Hammett that, while they enjoyed this or that novel or book of stories, they came away with a vague sense of disappointment, having expected something more startling, more sharply original from such a legendary writer. While they were, they admit, swept away in spite of themselves by certain scenes and sequences, they found themselves, at other times, with the uncomfortable feeling that they had heard this dialogue—or met this detective—somewhere before.

Such is the fate of being the first of the line. So numerous have Hammett's progeny been—indeed the whole subgenre of cops and robbers stories that still flourishes in our popular media was ushered in by Hammett's break with the tradition of detective fiction he inherited—that much of the stunning freshness which earlier readers encountered in his work has inevitably been lost. Hammett invented the modern urban detective story: its poses, its dialogue, its *rhythms,* its ethos, its heroes and villains. There was nothing like them before Hammett, and much of what has come after has been mere variations—however talented, however clever—on the forms he created.

It is, moreover, difficult to appreciate fully the impact Hammett's stories had on a generation whose anxious, colorful, naive and brutal, frantic and shell-shocked world he caught so perfectly. The special poignance of the new sense of vulnerability and peculiarly modern disillusionment with civilization many felt in the wake of World War I is difficult to imagine at half a century's remove— the way it must have felt to be embarking on the era of Prohibition not knowing, as we do now, that it would fail, indeed would usher in the reign of organized crime in America; the strange, unprecedented horror Americans, who had grown up with barbershop quartets and cotton candy, must have felt reading in their daily papers about machinegun slayings in city streets and massacres of rival gangs in closed garages. Hard, too, to imagine the giddy exhilaration—the sense of excitement and danger—that must have accompanied the coming of the automobile, the emancipation of young women from Victorian mores, the naughty but oddly compelling theories of a Viennese psychiatrist named Sigmund Freud. (Hammett's frankness with respect to such things helped give his work an edge that is lost now.)

I have tried, among other things, to describe the original context of Hammett's fiction in order to better understand the power it must have had for its first readers. If one cannot turn back the clock to 1929, one can at least try to repair some of the injustice done to an extraordinary body of work by three generations of imitators and the relentless march of time.

The other problem that confronts the modern reader of Hammett is quite opposite in character. One cannot help now but to read the stories in the context of the rest of the author's life—in particular, what we know about his politics and his suffering at the hands of McCarthyism during the fifties. In fact it was my curiosity about what sort of detective stories such a man might have written that led me, never having read a line of his fiction (though like most of my generation I had seen the movies), to undertake this book. I hasten to add that what I have written is in no sense a biography—several of which have recently appeared—although I have tried in some rough fashion to set the unfolding of Hammett's work against the backdrop of his life.

Nor have I made any attempt to consider all that has been written and thought about Hammett's fiction, though I have acknowledged my debts to certain writers. Rather, what I have striven to produce is a fresh look at the body of work Hammett left. I have found much that suggests that his writing—and his purposes—were far more artful, and far more carefully crafted, than is often conceded.

Since I was not interested in producing a scholarly exercise of interest only to specialists, I have chosen to discuss only works that are readily available to the average reader: the five novels and two collections of Hammett's shorter fiction currently in print. And, for the same reasons, when referring to Hammett's work in my notes, I have used the paperback editions.

An unprecedented amount of space—fully half the book—is devoted to Hammett's short fiction. It makes sense to do so. After all, fully half his career—the years from 1922 to 1929, when he was discovered by the American public at large—was spent "underground" writing stories for the so-called "pulp" magazines, chiefly one with the very fin de siècle name of *Black Mask*. It was here that Hammett honed his craft as a writer and first explored many of the themes, techniques, and fictional situations that were to preoccupy him throughout his career. The much better known novels are seen in a new light, I believe, when examined as part of this continuum.

Readers who are annoyed by such things are forewarned that, while I have tried not to spoil too many of the surprises of Hammett's denouements, I have found it necessary in a number of cases (particularly where the novels are concerned) to reveal names of murderers and/or solutions. It has been said that Hammett's greatest innovation was that he wrote detective stories which were worth reading even if the last page was missing. True enough. In a certain sense, that is the whole premise of this book. Hammett's stories command our attention not with the startling revelations on the final page but with the many smaller revelations of a far more interesting sort strewn like so many crumbs of bread along the way—as though finding his way back to the person he was that morning is as important to Hammett's hero as finding his way to the heart of the crime.

For it was in the work of Dashiell Hammett that the fictional detective reached self-consciousness. Before Hammett, the emphasis—for all the eccentricities of character indulged for the amusement of the reader—was on the solving of the crime. With Hammett, the detective himself—his aches and pains, his motives, values, feelings, and needs, his fears of growing old—has become the real subject. The people with whom he deals fascinate him as much as the evil deed he is investigating. As does his own behavior. Hammett invested his fictions not only with a gift for memorable writing but also with an extraordinary feel for the human condition and a series of questions that lie at the heart of the twentieth-century experience: Is it still possible to be a good person in what is manifestly an evil world? Wherein, given the collapse of the traditional shared value system, does that goodness consist? (In other words, how can we continue to tell the difference between the good folks and the bad folks?) How do we know what we know? And is it possible to live a life without trusting in something or someone?

In their characteristic blend of cynicism and idealism Hammett's fictional heroes mirror what seems to have been their creator's lifelong struggle with his own contradictory behavior. The perennial themes of guilt and punishment found in all detective stories are complicated, in Hammett's, by all the ambiguities and maddening uncertainties that haunt the real world. What makes Hammett's heroes interesting is not, finally, their endearing tough talk or the steel nerves with which they face their nemeses, nor even their touching moments of odd vulnerability (a lifelong theme of Hammett's), but the fact that they experience doubt, guilt, the judgment of time, a yearning to believe in someone or something, revulsion toward their own actions, the need for forgiveness and—especially in the case of Sam Spade and the Continental Op—a real agony over what is happening to their humanity.

Hammett's deeper concerns, in other words, are essentially spiritual in nature—a fact that has not sufficiently been noted, though everybody talks about his sense of honor and of the importance of commitment to a code. The present book follows this concern with spiritual issues, and what can only be described as the moral perspective, through Hammett's entire career—from his early days as a fallen-away Catholic of some ferocity to his later years as a communist manqué and patriot rejected by his own country.

Hounded and harrassed by the Internal Revenue Service and various government committees through the last sickly years of his life, unable to write, and having turned away finally even from the solace of alcohol, Hammett clung to the same deeply rooted convictions—and demonstrated the same qualities of character—that had informed his craft and sullen art. As a writer he had asked important questions, and ventured some bold answers . . . and showed us things about our society and our very language—the way we talk and think about our lives—that have become a permanent part of what we know.

But perhaps the most remarkable thing of all about Dashiell Hammett is that he managed to accomplish all of these things in the course of turning out some of the best detective stories anybody ever wrote.

D.D.
Cleveland, Ohio
July 1984

1
Hell's Pavement: The Unintended Era

"Everybody calls me a racketeer. I call myself a businessman."

—*Al Capone to a reporter*

It is a moment so turned-inside-out in its imagery—like a photographic negative trading light for darkness, darkness for light—that it haunts our reading, decades later, of his books, written decades before: Dashiell Hammett at fifty-seven, gaunt and white-haired, descending unsteadily on a cold December day in 1951 from the airplane that was returning him to society after five months in prison. "The invalid figure was trying to walk proud," remembers Lillian Hellman in her autobiography, "but coming down the ramp from the plane he was holding tight to the railing, and before he saw me he stumbled and stopped to rest."

Summoned before the U.S. 2nd District Court the previous July, Hammett had gone to jail rather than reveal the names on a list of contributors to the Civil Rights Congress bail bond fund, of which he was a trustee. The truth of the matter was that Hammett had never seen the list, had never even been in the organization's office. It was a simple question of principle, he explained to his anguished friend Lillian Hellman. His refusal to cooperate, even tacitly, as had so many of his talented Hollywood friends for the sake of their careers, had "something to do," he said, "with keeping my word."

A self-confessed Communist, Hammett frequently admitted to Hellman that "a great deal about Communism worried him." He had taken as much flak from the leftist press for his non-party-line novels as he had from the red-baiters for his socialist sympathies. He had enlisted in the armed services during both world wars. The second time, he had talked his way in when age (he was forty-eight) and the scars on his lungs should have disqualified him for service and had taken a demotion from sergeant to private. A man who in every other part of his life "always had to have things on his own terms," Hammett seemed to Hellman to have been oddly "happy" in the army. Stationed in the lonely and frozen Aleutians with a small band of griping youngsters half his age, he uncomplainingly carried out his assignment, editing a dull army paper. In prison, in his fifties, he conscientiously performed what many men would have considered a degrading job, scouring the cell-block lavatories.

Going to jail during the Cold War years was merely another way of serving his country—by standing up for its ideals in a time when its elected representatives had misplaced them. An even deeper motivation, thinks social historian Garry Wills, was Hammett's concern with upholding "a private kind of honor in a rotten world." Hammett's fierce personal integrity was felt by those who knew him. The prison guards instinctively addressed him as "sir."

The years of money and success when he had been lionized by the elite of Hollywood and New York—all behind him now—had been characterized by great binges of prodigal spending and drinking alternating with periods of awesome discipline and self-denial. He gave his money away to practically anybody who asked him for it, right on down to and including bums and pitiable frauds, and, on occasion, something he considered a precious possession to somebody who "wanted it more" than he did. Almost like a monk who sought to purge himself of hunger for material things, he withdrew into an ever more austere asceticism.

But the harsh experience of prison, says Hellman, took a terrible toll. Jail had left "a thin man thinner, a sick man sicker." As Hammett had once supported her during her lean years as a play-

wright, she now supported him while his ever-poor health deterio-
rated even further. Ten unproductive and difficult years later, Samuel Dashiell Hammett would be dead of the lung disease—finally
complicated by cancer—that had plagued him all his life.

He had been born in St. Mary's County, Maryland, between the
Potomac and Patuxent Rivers, on May 27, 1894, to Annie Bond and
Richard Thomas Hammett, two southern Catholics of French and
Scottish ancestry. His middle name was an Americanized version
of De Chiel, an old family name on the French side. Though he was
later to turn away from it, Hammett's youthful experience of his
family's religion seems to have had the same deep and enduring
effect it has had on other youngsters whose minds were marked by a
passionate idealism. Hellman elsewhere describes a very touching
scene, many years later, in which Hammett, "a bitter ex-Catholic,"
sat on the terrace steps of their farmhouse in Westchester County
with their farmer's chubby small son, "taking the boy through his
catechism and explaining with sympathy the meaning of the cere-
mony."

One senses that this incident may be an important key to the
man. A passionate Marxist, he found himself unable to swallow the
party line; a patriotic American, he went to jail rather than comply
with an instruction from his government that went against his
conscience. Even in his friendships with individuals, notes Hellman,
Hammett's ferocious concern with honesty always took precedence
over keeping peace or stroking somebody's ego, "as if one lie would
muck up his world."

As a teenager, threatened with being fired from his job with the
Baltimore and Ohio Railroad unless he could give his word that he
would never be late for work again, Hammett told his boss he was
sorry, but he couldn't do that, and picked up his cap to go. (His
superior quickly changed his mind and asked him to stay.)

Having dropped out of Baltimore Polytechnic Institute soon
after beginning his first year of high school, Hammett worked
around the railroad yards for a time as a freight clerk, a stevedore, a
timekeeper and a yardman; later as a laborer and a nail-machine
operator in a box factory. He was barely out of his teens when he
answered a want ad placed by the Pinkerton Detective Bureau,
which was hiring detectives. Sent out on all manner of assignments

from transporting prisoners and shadowing suspects to recovering a stolen Ferris wheel, the young Hammett faced every kind of danger and challenge to his wily mind. He was soon picking up an intimate knowledge not only of police procedure but of the criminal trades, the favorite tricks and dodges of their practitioners and their often highly specialized—and colorful—argot. A *yegg* was a safecracker. A *paper-pusher* passed counterfeit money. A *sticker* was a warrant for somebody's arrest, a *buzzer* a badge. A *hophead* was a drug addict, and a *pill* could be either a shot of cocaine or a bullet.

One of the first magazine pieces he was ever to publish is little more than a string of pithy and often not unamusing jottings entitled "From the Memoirs of a Private Detective." Some examples: "Pocket-picking is the easiest to master of all the criminal trades. Anyone who is not crippled can become an adept in a day." "House burglary is probably the poorest paid trade in the world; I have never known anyone to make a living at it. But for that matter few criminals of any class are self-supporting unless they toil at something legitimate between times." "In 1917, in Washington, D.C., I met a young woman who did not remark that my work must be very interesting."

But it must in fact have been an enormously interesting lifestyle to a young man who, having had no formal education after grammar school, would throughout his life astound highly educated acquaintances with his voracious reading in the most arcane and improbable of subjects. Even as a young operative he would cock a bemused eyebrow over a fellow agency employee who changed "voracious" to "truthful" and "simulate" to "quicken" in Hammett's typed reports on the grounds that the clients might not understand his big words. Many of the memories recounted in his "Memoirs" reveal Hammett's fascination, even then, with irony and paradox. ("I know a forger who left his wife because she had learned to smoke cigarettes while he was serving a term in prison." "The cleverest and most uniformly successful detective I have ever known is extremely myopic.") But the scars from knife and bullet wounds that fascinated friends in high society in later years were not gotten reading books nights.

In June of 1918, with a war raging in Europe, Hammett left Pinkerton's to enlist in the Motor Ambulance Corps. To his great disappointment he was stationed at a camp barely twenty miles from his hometown of Baltimore. While another ambulance driver named Ernest Hemingway already lay reading love letters that fall—even as an armistice agreement was being signed in Field Marshall Foch's railroad car near Compeigne, France—from a young nurse named Agnes von Kurowsky, whom he had met in the Ospedale Croce Rossa Americana in Milan while recuperating from a machine-gun wound, and whom he would later immortalize as the tragic Catherine Barkley in *A Farewell to Arms* (1929), Hammett was bedridden with a savage bout of influenza. (It was the same epidemic that would eventually claim twenty-seven million lives worldwide during that fall and winter and would keep a frustrated young Princeton graduate named F. Scott Fitzgerald, whose own warzone-bound regiment was down sick at a camp on Long Island, from seeing action "over there.") The influenza gave way to tuberculosis.

Mustered out of the army the following July, Hammett got his old job back at Pinkerton's, which soon had him tailing popular entertainer Fanny Brice in connection with some accusations made concerning her notorious second husband, the inveterate gambler and Wall Street con man Nickie Arnstein. A variety of other assignments over the next several months took Hammett around the country in the pursuit of missing persons, evidence and felons. In *Dashiell Hammett: A Casebook* (McNally & Loftin, 1969), the first book-length study of Hammett's career, William F. Nolan recounts several amusing stories from Hammett's Pinkerton years, such as the time he spent three months in a hospital shadowing—and surreptitiously interrogating—a suspect in the next bed.

By the summer of 1920 Hammett was back in a hospital bed for real. His long work hours and run-down condition seem to have resulted in a recurrence of his tuberculosis. Confined to a veterans' hospital in a converted Indian school outside Tacoma, Washington, he whiled away the hours playing poker with the other inmates and drinking bootleg whiskey. (Alcohol had become officially illegal with the ratification of the eighteenth amendment and Volstead Act, which became effective on January 16th of that year.) His Pinkerton blackjack, which he kept in a drawer by his bed, was a popular conversation piece.

An incorrigible prankster who loved to pull the legs of the

hospital staff, Hammett was soon moved to an army hospital on the edge of the desert, near San Diego. There, to relieve the boredom, he took to staging gila monster—rattler fights ("The Gila monsters always won," he later observed, "but most of the sucker money backed the rattlers") and, as his health began to improve, took occasional weekend holidays over the border in nearby Tijuana.

The following May, his now chronic condition judged by the army doctors to have reached "maximum improvement," Hammett set out for San Francisco with his new wife Josephine Dolan, a nurse he had met at the hospital and married the previous December. Though his original intent seems to have been to stay in the city only a few weeks, Hammett was soon prowling its colorful neighborhoods on behalf of the local Pinkerton's branch office.

He would spend eight years in San Francisco, but his life there was to take a very different form from what he had at first anticipated. Within a year he would be living away from his wife and small daughter Mary Jane, holed up in a cheap downtown hotel room, living on soup, and trying to write. The truth is he had soured on detective work. An incident involving an Australia-bound ship out of San Francisco Harbor, which was believed to have $200,000 in missing gold hidden aboard, is generally credited with being the thing that finally tore it for Hammett. Hired to recover the loot, which previous searches had failed to turn up, he was beginning to warm up to the idea of a trip to Australia and had packed his things per instructions from Pinkerton's and stowed them aboard the ship, which was about to sail, when, instinctively following up one last hunch, he climbed to the top of a smokestack and looked in: There was the missing gold. Furious with himself for not having waited until they were one day out at sea, he returned the loot to the agency—along with his resignation.

What really seems to have happened to Hammett was that the adventure and challenge he had first found in detective work had gradually been outweighed by the sordid side of his profession. The endless examples of greed, dishonesty and deception—Hammett himself was continually having to pass himself off as someone else, to take advantage of other people's credulity and instinctive trust in him—must have been hard on a man of his innate integrity. The experience of being used by clients, especially the wealthy or powerful, to control other people must have been harder still. In conversations with Lillian Hellman in later years he would refer cynically to his role as having sometimes been that of a hired thug. "No," he once snapped to her protests that a certain relative of hers, the owner of a fruit company in Central America, was not a murderer, "he just hired people to do it for him. I was in that racket for a lot of years and I don't like it."

He was referring to the fact that Pinkerton agents were occasionally hired by industry to help break strikes. The plot of Hammett's novel *Red Harvest* may well have been suggested by the widespread strikes by coal miners that had occurred following a disastrous drop in coal prices in 1921, prompting mine owners to cut pay. Many miners, as a result, called for nationalization of the industry. Such strikes were bitter and hard-fought, as newly formed unions gained strength among workers and put pressure on management for reforms. Owners who were not in the habit of being told what to do by their employees were frequently not above using any means available to them to defuse or divide the opposition.

Hammett confided to Hellman on another occasion that an officer of the Anaconda Copper Company had once offered him $5,000 to kill union organizer Frank Little. When Little was subsequently lynched along with three other men, Hammett was filled with revulsion—both against a society whose pervasive corruption was becoming ever more evident and oppressive to him, and toward himself, that his behavior or general willingness to carry out his client's wishes had given the official the impression he would execute any assignment.

Years later, when his good friend William Faulkner kept insisting that his popular and somewhat salacious novel *Sanctuary* was a "potboiler" he had written only for the money, Hammett was equally adamant in his position that "nobody ever deliberately wrote a potboiler, you just did the best you could and woke up to find it good or no good." You took responsibility for what you did in this life, and that was all there was to it. For Hammett, his occasional role as a paid thug had become intolerable.

So at twenty-seven, as his worsening lung ailment began to make him think that he would not live long, he took a subsistence-level job writing advertising copy for a San Francisco jeweler named

Albert S. Samuels (whose name, along with those of several of his employees, would later turn up in one form or another in his books—young Peggy O'Toole's as the name of a racehorse in *The Glass Key*). Dashiell Hammett holed up in his rented room to write. Poems and squibs soon appeared in a number of magazines, the most notable among them probably being H. L. Mencken and George Jean Nathan's *The Smart Set*. And he sold his first story, in 1922, to a periodical called *Brief Stories*.

It was a detective story entitled "The Barber and His Wife." In the following year, 1923, he would sell fourteen stories, most of them already showing the hard, unsentimental style that was to revolutionize detective fiction over the next decade. Seven of them appeared in a popular, if somewhat tawdry, magazine called *The Black Mask*.

Launched in the summer of 1920 by the very same pair of ambitious men of letters who edited the more pretentious *Smart Set*, *The Black Mask* was a frank attempt on the part of Mencken and Nathan to turn a fast buck by pandering directly to the fast-growing audience for sensational "pulp" fiction. A number of such magazines had sprung up in the years before World War One, the heirs of such popular dime novels as Ned Buntline's highly exaggerated "true life" adventures of Buffalo Bill Cody, more or less apocryphal autobiographies of late nineteenth-century outlaw heroes like Belle Starr and Jesse James; the dashing exploits of fictional Yale athlete Frank Merriwell; and the enormously successful Horatio Alger books, 118 in all, which sold 250 million copies.

The national demand for escapist literature had risen steadily as the financial depression of 1895, the rising turmoil and discontent among overcrowded, crime-ridden cities, the violence of the labor scene with its increasingly numerous lockouts and bloody strikes, and finally the unprecedented global violence of the First World War made life more anxious and frustrating. By 1910 something like ten million Americans a week were flocking to neighborhood vaudeville houses and nickelodeons to gape at something called "movies." By the middle of the decade the soundless comedies of Mack Sennett and Charlie Chaplin and the sprawling epics of D. W. Griffith had launched a new industry. The western was taken over from "realists" like Zane Grey, notes social historian Tony Goodstone in *The Pulps*, and given its present-day mythic dimension by bestselling author Max Brand.

The public craved larger-than-life fiction and supercharged emotional highs. The pulps—with names like *Astounding Stories, Weird Tales, Spicy Mystery Stories,* and *Wild West Weekly*—filled that need. Printed on cheap paper and selling for anywhere from ten cents to twenty-five, they packed between their lurid covers a taste-defying diet of neo-Gothic romances and love stories, bloody tales of the occult, overwritten detective stories and shoot-em-up sagebrush sagas, delightfully sinister tales of Fu Manchu evil, and slightly warped adventure stories in which women were regularly humiliated and occasionally forced to undress by misshapen fiends.

But out of this distinctly unpromising brew came Edgar Rice Burroughs's stories of Tarzan of the Apes (1912), which were to become, in Goodstone's words, "the major influence on adventure fiction, science-fiction and related forms for at least twenty years," and Earl Derr Biggers's inscrutable Chinese sleuth Charlie Chan. ("Can nothing be done?" the man standing over the body of a slain woman asks Chan in a 1932 story. "Can the fallen flower return to the branch again?" the detective philosophizes.) And *Black Mask*— the article was dropped from its title later—was to count among its more illustrious alumni Erle Stanley Gardner, Dashiell Hammett and Raymond Chandler.

It takes "a very open mind indeed," wrote Chandler (whose first *Black Mask* story appeared a full decade after Hammett's) in his essay "The Simple Art of Murder," "to look beyond the unnecessarily gaudy covers, trashy titles and barely acceptable advertisements [of the pulps] and recognize the authentic power of a kind of writing that, even at its most mannered and artificial, made most of the fiction of the time taste like a cup of luke-warm consomme at a spinsterish tearoom." Nor did he feel this special power was "entirely a matter of violence, although far too many people got killed in these stories and their passing was celebrated with rather too loving attention to detail."

> It certainly was not a matter of fine writing, since any attempt at that would have been ruthlessly blue-penciled by the editorial staff. Nor was it because of any great originality of plot or character. Most of the

plots were rather ordinary and most of the characters rather primitive types of people. Possibly it was the smell of fear which these stories managed to generate. Their characters lived in a world gone wrong, a world in which, long before the atom bomb, civilization had created the machinery for its own destruction, and was learning to use it with all the moronic delight of a gangster trying out his first machine gun. The law was something to be manipulated for profit and power. The streets were dark with something more than night.

Behind its cockiness and chic cynicism, the decade in which Dashiell Hammett sat down to write was a restless, troubled period of social upheaval and an increasingly nervous excitement: an era that began with the winning of women's suffrage and the "Noble Experiment" of Prohibition and ended with the St. Valentine's Day Massacre and the Crash of '29, the result of a prolonged binge of overextended buying. Despite President Harding's calm assurance of a return to normalcy, post-World War One America would never be the same. The infamous "Teapot Dome" Scandal that rocked his paternalistic administration (1921–23) and the widespread political corruption that followed the coming of Prohibition seriously eroded the public's confidence in its leaders, while the rise of advertising gaily hawked shares in a dream world whose days were already numbered.

Jazz, an exhilarating new music spreading outward from the south, and the proliferation of radio, dance halls and automobiles (fewer than seven million in 1920 to 23 million by the end of the decade) were effecting a revolution in lifestyle. It is difficult at this remove in time to appreciate the incredible impact of the automobile on American society. It made possible almost overnight the modern-day getaway—whether one was a stickup man fleeing the police or a fledgling entrepreneur running illegal booze down dark country roads—and the exciting chase scenes that quickly became one of Hollywood's staples. The black sedan with its quick-strike capability was as crucial an element in gang warfare as the machineguns and other weapons that became available after the war.

But the automobile's impact on the non-criminal element of society was equally great. It created a vastly increased mobility that was at once exhilarating and scary. It offered, writes Frederick Lewis Allen, "an almost universally available means of escaping temporarily from the supervision of parents and chaperons"—a situation underlying several of Hammett's stories—"or from the influence of neighborhood opinion. Boys and girls now thought nothing . . . of jumping into a car and driving off at a moment's notice—without asking anybody's permission—to a dance in another town twenty miles away, where they were strangers and enjoyed a freedom impossible among their neighbors." The closed car was something else again.

Only 10 per cent of American automobiles produced in 1919 had been closed. By 1924, it was 43 per cent; and by 1927, 82.8. It "was in effect a room protected from the weather," says Allen, "which could be occupied at any time of the day or night and could be moved at will into a darkened byway or a country lane." The increased possibilities for deviltry it offered the rebellious youngster was not lost on a troubled generation of Victorian parents.

Young women who had held down "men's jobs" in wartime factories, and now commanded the vote into the bargain, rebelled at the old dispensation—ankle-length dresses, heavy woolen stockings, and sober hairdos gave way to lipstick, bobbed hair, short skirts and smoking cigarettes *in public*. Doing the Charleston and the Black Bottom and shocking one's elders were in. The double bombshell dropped by F. Scott Fitzgerald's runaway bestseller *This Side of Paradise* in 1920 was the unabashed depiction of the fact that American youth were not only having sex, they were *talking* about it, too.

In this Brave New World disturbing social issues were bubbling to the surface. The brilliant trial lawyer Clarence Darrow defended both Leopold and Loeb, two millionaires' sons from the university who had killed a young boy as a "scientific" experiment (Darrow opposed capital punishment), and a Dayton teacher named Scopes, who had been fired for teaching Darwin's theory of evolution—this in 1925, the same year *The Great Gatsby* was published. Elsewhere, a German politician named Adolf Hitler was already beginning his slow ominous rise, while thousands wept, the following summer, at the funeral of a hokey movie star named Rudolph Valentino, and, the summer after that, even greater crowds hysterically cheered a slim, sandy-haired airmail pilot standing on the deck of the presidential battle cruiser that had carried him home from France.

Against this background, Dashiell Hammett's stories took shape and reached their first limited public. It was only with the publication of his first hardcover novels in 1929 that he received any critical attention or for that matter became known to the public at large. His last novel, *The Thin Man,* debuted in magazine form in 1933, the same year Prohibition was repealed. Though this is probably a mere coincidence, it is an unusually poetic one. While Fitzgerald had taken as his domain the jazzy world of the social-climbing new affluent society, and Sinclair Lewis the foibles and moral bankruptcy of small-town America, Hammett had decided to write about the milieu he knew best, the world of crime. But his criminals were not the cultivated villains of Agatha Christie's or Dorothy Sayers's novels, nor the Professor Moriaritys of Conan Doyle's. They were mostly the slightly crazed punks and anxious junkies of the twenties underworld, the corrupt politicians and opportunists of the derailed American Dream.

In January 1920 a euphoric Anti-Saloon League proclaimed the start of "an era of clear thinking and clean living." Instead, Prohibition ushered in a decade of unparalleled crime and corruption. Judges and law-enforcement officers lined up for their share of the enormous profits made from bootleg whiskey and beer—a nefarious industry controlled by rival and frequently clashing gangs. In Chicago alone, in one four-year period, two hundred twenty-seven gangsters were murdered without a single conviction, while large numbers of civilians and prohibition agents also fell victim to gangland violence. Speakeasies, stills, hip flasks and bathtub gin were everywhere.

The rampant hypocrisy of the situation was not lost on the criminals. "Everybody calls me a racketeer," Al Capone once complained. "I call myself a businessman. When I sell liquor it's bootlegging. When my patrons serve it on a silver tray on Lake Shore Drive, it's hospitality." The hypocrisy was not lost on Hammett either. Though many of his stories involve criminals connected either directly or peripherally with bootlegging and his detective is sometimes mistaken, as Hammett himself had been, for a prohibition agent—indeed his heroes are not above an illegal drink—bootleggers as such are never the objects of his pursuit, but only when they have become involved in other crimes such as murder.

Capone, who surveyed his dominions from the back seat of an armor-plated Cadillac, was said to have been implicated in four hundred murders. He had been called in from New York in 1920 as a young (twenty-three-year-old) turk by the Chicago bootlegger Johnny Torrio to help Torrio solidify his lucrative business interests. Capone soon assembled his own army of some seven hundred gunmen; by 1925 he controlled the suburb of Cicero, down to its mayor, its many gambling casinos and all one hundred sixty-one of its bars, and was well on his way to becoming the unchallenged czar of Chicago's underworld. The funeral of his chief rival, mobster Dion O'Bannion, drew twenty thousand mourners—among them several prominent judges and aldermen—and twenty-six truckloads of flowers including an extravagant wreath from Capone, whose men had gunned down O'Bannion in his florist shop per instructions from their boss. The card read simply, "From Al."

Such a world was light years, in its cold cynicism and brutal realities, from the fog-shrouded, cloak-and-dagger detective stories typical of the pulps when Mencken and Nathan, happy to be rid of the thing, sold *Black Mask* in 1921. Under the new editor, George W. Sutton, Jr., and his successors, Phil Cody (1924–1926) and Joseph Thompson "Cap" Shaw, who is credited with buying Chandler's first story in 1933, the magazine was to become the main vehicle for a whole new kind of detective fiction—the so-called hard-boiled or "tough guy" story. If Hammett was not the first to write this type of tale—that credit should perhaps go to his fellow contributor Carroll John Daly—he was unquestionably its leading exponent and guiding genius, the writer chiefly responsible for forging a fresh set of literary conventions—an approach to dialogue, character and motivation, a tone—that was adequate to the task of describing twentieth-century urban crime, the individuals who perpetrated it, and the men who made their living cleaning up after it.

But even as the young ex-Pinkerton detective was thrilling *Black Mask*'s "underground" readers with an entirely new kind of detective story, the vast reading public was devouring another type. The popular series of Nick Carter books begun before the turn of the century by Frederick van Rensselaer, whose plodding detective has been described as "possibly the blandest hero ever created," had been eclipsed in the years after World War I by the more playful, and infinitely cleverer, adventures of an egocentric little Belgian named Hercule Poirot (who had debuted in Agatha Christie's *The Mysterious Affair at Styles* in 1920); a dashing gentleman scholar with what Edmund Wilson once called the "embarrassing" name of Lord Peter Wimsey (introduced in Dorothy Sayers's *Whose Body?* in 1923); and their American cousin, Philo Vance.

The creation of Willard Huntington Wright, who recounted the supposedly authentic cases ("the most astonishing secret documents in American police history") in the persona of a close confidant and Watson figure named S. S. Van Dine, Vance was the bane of criminal kind and the delight of whodunit fans from 1926 *(The Benson Murder Case)* to 1933 when Wright was killed in an automobile accident. The well-to-do scion of a family of New York patricians, Vance merely dabbled in criminal cases at the behest of a distraught district attorney out of a detached intellectual curiosity.

"An aristocrat by birth and instinct, he held himself aloof from the world of men," a worshipful Van Dine informs the reader in *The Benson Murder Case*. "In his manner there was an indefinable contempt for inferiority of all kinds. The great majority of those with whom he came in contact regarded him as a snob." Bored, supercilious, condescending, a cynic given to sleeping late and smoking perfumed, rose-petal-tipped cigarettes called Regies and breakfasting in his dressing gown, the unpredictable Vance might one moment astonish his house guests with "an impromptu *causerie* . . . on Tanagra figurines, which, had it been transcribed, would have made a most delightful and instructive monograph," and in the next dazzle his readers with his virtuoso displays of deductive reasoning, while the police plumbed ever profounder depths of ineptitude.

This was the reigning image of the arch detective even as several carloads of slain mobster Dion O'Bannion's men sprayed hundreds of bullets into the storefront of Al Capone's headquarters in broad daylight. "He was unusually good-looking," says Van Dine of his doughty hero,

> although his mouth was ascetic and cruel, like the mouths on some of the Medici portraits; moreover, there was a slightly derisive hauteur in the lift of his eyebrows. Despite the aquiline severity of his lineaments his face was highly sensitive. His forehead was full and sloping—it was the artist's, rather than the scholar's, brow. His cold, grey eyes were

widely spaced. His nose was straight and slender, and his chin narrow but prominent, with an unusually deep cleft. When I saw John Barrymore recently in *Hamlet* I was somehow reminded of Vance; and once before, in a scene of *Caesar and Cleopatra* played by Forbes-Robertson [sic], I received a similar impression.

Consider, by way of contrast, the description Hammett's detective gives of himself in 1927 story "The Big Knockover":

> I'm short and lumpy. My face doesn't scare children, but it's a more or less truthful witness to a life that hasn't been over-burdened with refinement and gentility.

The difference went deeper than looks. Hammett's character, who had come to life in the pages of *Black Mask*, was the forerunner of Sam Spade and every other tough-talking, no-nonsense detective from Philip Marlowe to Baretta. An improbable hero at first glance, he was a stocky, middle-aged operative who worked out of the San Francisco office of the mythical Continental Detective Agency (which, coincidentally, was located at the same address as that city's Pinkerton branch office).

The Continental Op, as he became known to the magazine's avid readers, was never to have a proper name. Hammett had not planned it that way, he admitted in a letter to *Black Mask*'s editor, George W. Sutton, Jr., but having found he had written two stories about him without having had the occasion to come up with one, he decided it might be fun to keep it that way. His detective was, after all, a deliberate departure from the self-conscious, posturing sleuth of the Philo Vance mold. Hammett saw him more as "a type," a new kind of working-class hero who labored in anonymity at his often unglamorous, frequently tedious profession. To him detection was a job like any other job, with its dull days, its routine investigations and endless checking out of facts, its crummy hours and crummy pay, its occasional moments of satisfaction. "The private detective who is oftenest successful," wrote Hammett, is "neither the derby-hatted and broad-toed blockhead of one school of fiction, nor the all-knowing, infallible genius of another. I've worked with several of him."

In the Op, Hammett had set out to recreate on paper a true-to-life detective of the sort he had known during his eight years with

Pinkerton's. (Indeed, he maintained some years later that he had modeled him on a man named James Wright, an assistant superintendent he had known at the agency's Baltimore office.) The cases he investigated were to be realistic, his methods those actually used by the nine-to-five detectives of the real world.

Reviewing *The Benson Murder Case* in January 1927, Hammett ridiculed the story's "preposterous" solution, which revealed an ignorance of elementary ballistics and regular police procedure. "The authorities, no matter how stupid the author chose to make them, would have cleared up the mystery promptly if they had been allowed to follow the most rudimentary police routine," wrote Hammett. "But then what would there have been for the gifted Vance to do?" Van Dine's policemen, he complained, are hamstrung from the start.

> He doesn't let them ask any questions that aren't wholly irrelevant. They can't make inquiries of any one who might know anything. They aren't permitted to take any steps toward learning whether the dead man was robbed. Their fingerprint experts are excluded from the scene of the crime. When information concerning a mysterious box of jewelry accidentally bobs up everybody resolutely ignores it, since it would have led to a solution before the three-hundredth page.

Hammett's stories, by contrast, were to be full of authentic details drawn from his own years in the profession.

They would all be told, moreover, in the first person, a practice which initially must have caused some confusion among *Black Mask*'s readers, as the October 15, 1923, issue carried two Op stories—the second and third to appear—one over the familiar byline of Peter Collinson, the pseudonym Hammett had used until then, the other over the new byline of Dashiell Hammett.

The first Op tale, a hard-boiled short subject entitled "Arson Plus," had been published in the October 1 issue under the Collinson byline, as had several other Hammett pieces in *Black Mask* and the periodical *Brief Stories*. Among the turn-of-the-century underworld, Hammett once explained, "Peter Collins" was slang for "a nobody." He would be "nobody's son." The young writer seems to have been saving his own name for his poetry, with which he hoped to make his real mark on the literary scene. Although Hammett

contributed "squibs and . . . poems" to Mencken's *Smart Set,* he
seems to have abandoned that youthful dream around this time. The
story "Slippery Fingers" (which is notable for describing a method
used by real criminals to fake finger prints) would be the last to
appear under the Collinson byline. "Crooked Souls" (reprinted in
the collection *The Big Knockover* as "The Gatewood Caper")
marked the official debut of Dashiell Hammett, mystery writer.

2
A New Kind of Detective: Four Stories of 1924

". . . shivering and shaking in my wet clothes, keeping my mouth clamped tight so that my teeth wouldn't sound like a dice-game, I climbed into a taxi. . . ."

The Continental Op in "The Tenth Clew"

Of the forty-six stories Hammett published in *Black Mask* between 1922 and 1931, no fewer than thirty-four feature the Continental Op—so strong was the reader demand for further adventures of this credible hero. All of them have been reprinted at one time or another in various paperback and hardcover collections. Several form sequences that, later revised, became Hammett's first three novels. Two paperback anthologies of Hammett's shorter work, *The Big Knockover* (Vintage Books, 1972; edited and with an introduction by Lillian Hellman) and *The Continental Op* (Vintage Books, 1974—not to be confused with a paperback collection of the same name published in 1945 with different stories) contain sixteen of the best.

Although they cannot be thought of as "books" in anything like the sense in which Hammett's later novels are books, these two collections of early work already reveal most of the themes and values, as well as many of the literary devices, to be found in the mature work. Hammett's distinctive style was forged in the pages of *Black Mask*.

The Continental Op, including a thoughtful introduction by Steven Marcus, contains with only a couple of exceptions earlier stories than those in *The Big Knockover,* so it makes some sense to begin there. "The Tenth Clew," the story that opens the volume, was published January 1, 1924. The sixth of the Op adventures, it was also, at 10,000 words, Hammett's most ambitious effort to date and—evidence of how highly his editors thought of it—his first "cover" mention. It is in its way the epitome of Hammett's early writing.

The Op has been sent for by a wealthy San Francisco industrialist named Leopold Gantvoort who believes his life to be in danger. Before the detective has even had a chance to interview his prospective employer, Gantvoort turns up slumped over the wheel of a stolen car on a dark street near Golden Gate Park, his head bashed in with a typewriter. Besides the murder weapon, eight mysterious clues—including a threatening letter signed "E. B.," two bullets marked with X's, a list containing five names and addresses, and the fact that the victim's collar buttons and left shoe were removed—are all the Op has to go on. The agency's not inconsiderable resources are put to work running down several tantalizing leads that actually "lead" nowhere, except to the conclusion that at least one of them was almost certainly faked. "That's our tenth clew," exclaims the Op suddenly, "—the one we're going to follow from now on."

This pausing in mid-narrative to summarize what he knows, often at more than one juncture in a story, is typical of the Op. On one level it serves the practical function of clarifying for the reader what has happened up to that point; on another level, it tells something about the methodical mind of Hammett's hero. He is a man for whom there is no such thing as an isolated fact. Probe long enough, he believes, and you will see how everything connects to something else. The Op is a keen observer of people. "The first thing you noticed about her were her eyes," he says of Ganvoort's fiancée, the lovely Creda Dexter. "They were large and deep and the color of amber, and their pupils were never at rest. Continuously they changed size, expanded and contracted—slowly at times, suddenly at others—ranging incessantly from the size of pinheads to an extent that threatened to blot out the amber irises."

He is not wasting space on a minor detail. For the Op a person's face, especially the eyes, is the key to his or her personality. Creda is no exception. "With the eyes for a guide," he continues, "you discovered that she was pronouncedly feline throughout. Her every movement was the slow, smooth, sure one of a cat; and the contours of her rather pretty face, the shape of her mouth, her small nose, the set of her eyes, the swelling of her brows, were all cat-like."

The language of the body, once one has become adept at reading it, can be highly informative, since it is often involuntary. Later, when Creda is questioned about her brother's whereabouts, the Op notes that the "restless black pupils spread out abruptly, as if they were about to overflow into the white areas of her eyes. That was the first clear indication of fear I had seen. But, outside of those tell-tale pupils, her composure was undisturbed."

He grows increasingly suspicious of her, following his instincts even though his assessment of her makes it difficult to suppose her guilt. The story that finally comes to light bears out what will be a major theme of Hammett's work: things are not always what they seem, nor people who they at first appear to be. Another preoccupation of Hammett's is also found at the heart of the crime: a woman exploiting a man's trusting feelings.

But the Op's pursuit of the truth, for all his experience and powers of observation, is not always sure-footed. "I knew that I had blundered . . . had played my hand wrong in trying to shake him down too quickly—in driving too directly at the point I was interested in," he admits in one instance. His assumption that he is safe in the crowd aboard the ferry—"my second mistake of the day"—gets him dumped into the freezing night waters of the bay. Hammett describes the moment of violence that overtakes his hero with characteristic indirection: "The entire back of my head burned with sudden fire . . . tiny points of light glittered in the blackness before me. . . ." The Op is a fallible, very human hero who almost surrenders to the soothing numbness of the waters, and injures his hand later when he throws a punch at his assailant. His tough language and hard-boiled imagery occasionally are thrown into odd

relief when they are juxtaposed with the spectacle of his vulnerability, as when he describes himself "shivering and shaking in my wet
clothes, keeping my mouth clamped tight so that my teeth wouldn't
sound like a dice game. . . ." It is not difficult to see how the readers
of *Black Mask* could become so attached to him.

In "The Golden Horseshoe" (first published in November 1924) the
Op has been working as a detective for fifteen years. Now in his
mid-thirties, he has grown a little weary of the "gun-play and other
forms of rioting." Engaged by a distraught Englishwoman to find her
dissolute wandering husband, a successful architect turned junkie
and social dropout—in order to "end this devilish uncertainty in
which she has been living"—he traces the man, one Norman
Ashcroft, to a little town on the other side of the Mexican border and
the saloon whose name gives the story its title.

The account is spiced with the kind of authentic touches a real
detective was able to supply, such as the way investigators deal with
bureaucrats like postal inspectors; the argot of the underworld
("I've got a line on a scratcher [check forger] from up north"); and
the knack of reading a man's character and putting it in a nutshell
that was fast becoming one of the hallmarks of Hammett's style.
When a nervous criminal type tries to pull a gun on him, the
detective knocks him to the floor and disarms him, then casually
turns his back on the fellow, resuming his seat at the corner of the
table. "He had only that one flash of fight in him," says the Op. "He
got up sniveling."

Hammett zeroes in on the character of Mrs. Ashcroft with the
same spare prose: "Clear was the word that best fit her." She
embodies what he likes in a woman—the same qualities that he likes
in any person. "Mrs. Ashcroft held a *strong, slender* hand out to
me," he writes, and later says of her, "She grinned at me—a grin
that was as boyish as the *straight* look of her brown eyes" (italics
mine). Hammett might be discussing his own prose style, and the
values in that regard which he shares with Hemingway. The man the
Op finds in the Mexican saloon embodies the opposite qualities:
"Not altogether on the rocks yet, but you could see evidence of the
down-hill slide plainly in the *dullness* of his blue eyes . . . in the
blurred lines around his mouth and the mouth's *looseness*" (italics

mine). On the other hand, the Op's self-conscious conversation at the bar with a "lanky girl who had done something to her hair that made it purple" reveals a soft spot for floozies.

His own lapses are obviously meant to be similarly endearing: he trips on a gun at a particularly inopportune moment, and excuses himself from the scene of a brutal multiple murder even as he rationalizes his feelings.

> Then I went out of the front door and sat on the top step, smoking a cigarette while I waited for the police.
>
> I felt rotten. I've seen dead people in larger quantities than three in my lifetime, but this thing had fallen on me while my nerves were ragged from three days of boozing.

Again, in this story, Hammett shows feelings—in this case a character's determination—indirectly through a description of physical features ("His eyes were hard and cold and his mouth was shut until you could hardly see the slit of it"). He also fastens on a person's most telling feature as a kind of shorthand for evoking the whole personality—as when he returns again and again to the opaque, shark-like eyes of the menacing Gooseneck Flinn, Ashcroft's strongarm accomplice: "His eyes were black shoe-buttons stuck close together at the top of a little mashed nose." And later: "His face was thrust forward to the full length of his long, yellow neck. His shoe-button eyes focused on me." Even if these early stories show a tendency to overuse the imagery of eyes, few writers have been able to ring so many changes on one feature with such consistent effectiveness.

On the train back to San Francisco the Op takes time out to make his usual "list of what I knew and guessed about Norman Ashcroft, alias Ed Bohannon." The guesses are as much a part of his approach as his rehearsal of the facts, for Hammett's detective sees his work as a kind of game—poker imagery abounds in the stories— that must be played out one move, one hand at a time. "My game just now," he confides at one point, "was to persuade Ed and his girl to bolt." The reader is meant to enjoy his ingenious strategies in this story just as he is meant to enjoy his occasional wisecracks and the breathlessly sketched action scenes that occur in each of his stories and that were to make him a natural for Hollywood.

But once again the Op is revealed as no simple character. If he sees himself as something of a poker player at life, he also exhibits the moral man's concern for truth and resentment of obfuscation. "I was trying to count how many lies could be found in those nine words," he says, killing time with an advertisement that hangs over the bar. And getting to the bottom of the crime proves once again to be a matter of peeling away false identities: the reader is continually reminded that people are not always who or what they seem. An identity can itself be a mask. In this light, it becomes increasingly interesting that the Op himself chooses to forgo one, preferring to be known by his actions or the occasional reference to him simply as "our stout friend" or "Shorty."

A new theme is in evidence here as well: his concern for justice, or, more precisely, with a sense of balance that must be maintained. If a man cannot be hanged for a murder he did commit, let him be hanged for one he didn't commit, says the Op, "so justice won't be cheated."

On another level, "Horseshoe" shows us a writer who is having an increasingly difficult time doing justice to his subtle themes and complex notions of character in the limited format of the short story. The story leaves the impression of a tale that might have been spun out in a more leisurely manner, by dramatizing the large chunks of compressed narrative in which background is filled in. One of the things that fascinates Hammett is the way in which one action eventually leads, far down the line, to another—which is the stuff of novels. In any case, his growing restlessness with the short form is even more evident in the next two stories (actually published in *Black Mask* earlier that year), which are connected in the form of a sequence.

At thirty, Hammett has already perfected a style of stunning economy. He writes like the Op thinks, cutting through the irrelevant and moving swiftly to the business at hand. Digressions are almost nonexistent. The stories open, typically, in medias res, with the Op already caught up in the new adventure. "I had been told that the man for whom I was hunting lived in a certain Turk Street block," begins the first sentence of "The House in Turk Street." But this tale is to be a departure from the usual pattern of the detective story, which works from the outside from the residue of clues and effects toward the turbulent center where desperate actions take place as the truth becomes known and the avenues of escape closed off. Only three pages into this strange adventure the Op finds himself suddenly at dead center, smack in the middle of a sinister situation that has nothing to do with the assignment he is on, helpless and the prisoner of a ruthless gang who think he knows something he does not.

Ironically, it is his basically moral nature, which occasionally leaves him off balance, that delivers the Op into their clutches. He instinctively trusts the sweet old couple at whose door he has knocked to ask questions. When he gives the fake name he has used with the other residents of the block he comes "as near blushing . . . as I have in fifteen years. These folks weren't made to be lied to." Indeed the usually canny detective is so thoroughly taken in by their act that he is caught totally off guard by the cold touch of a gun muzzle on the back of his neck as he is having a peaceful smoke in one of their living-room chairs. When a voice orders him to stand up, the narration continues: "I didn't stand up: I couldn't. I was paralyzed. I sat and blinked at the Quarres." The gang—which includes the old couple—has been watching him asking questions up and down the street and is sure he is after them. But what follows, by way of redeeming himself, is a virtuoso display of his ability to read people and figure out what they are up to.

At first all he has to go on is the voices of the others in the next room who converse, or argue rather, with Hook, the man who is holding a gun on him. The Op rapidly deduces their relationships, their vulnerabilities, the ways they play one another off against the other.

> [Hook's] ugly face grew warm and red and utterly happy, and he took a deep breath and straightened his shoulders. In his place, I might have believed her myself—all of us have fallen for that thing at one time or another—but sitting tied up on the side-lines, I knew that he'd have been better off playing with a gallon of nitro than with this baby. She was dangerous! There was a rough time ahead for Hook.

One by one they enter the room: the young woman with her "smoke-gray eyes . . . set too far apart for trustworthiness" and her "little sharp animal-teeth"; the short, fat Chinese "immaculately clothed in garments that were as British as his accent," with his "little opaque eyes that were like two black seeds," "eyes that were as hard and black and inhuman as two pieces of coal." "His face was a round yellow mask," notes the detective, "and his voice was the same emotionless drawl that I had heard before; but I knew that he was as surely under the girl's sway as the ugly man—or he wouldn't have let her taunt bring him into the room. But I doubted that she'd find this Anglicized Oriental as easily handled as Hook." The Op's self-description, meanwhile, has the effect of heightening his own vulnerability in the eyes of the reader: "She laughed at me—a fat man, all trussed up with red plush rope, and with the corner of a green cushion in my mouth. . . ."

Even as he measures their mutual distrust, his keen habits of observation tell him a doublecross is in progress: the bag of loot from the gang's recent heist is not where it was a few moments before. "The girl had stirred up the trouble between the two men to distract their attention while she made a switch." Then, as the action begins to accelerate, he suddenly perceives he is to be the hapless weapon with which the two men are to play out their duel. For the next few pages his mind races through what he knows about them, anticipating each of their moves and counter moves—and what they expect he will do. Using their insecurity and suspicion, he plays one off against the other like the cunning gamester he is. "I grinned into his round yellow face," says the Op, "and led my ace. . . .

"His face showed nothing, but I imagined that his fat body stiffened a little within its fashionable British clothing. That encouraged me, and I went on"—upping the ante—"with my little lie that was meant to stir things up."

The game is survival.

"I got up from my seat . . . and moved cautiously to a spot that I thought would be out of the line of fire if the thing I expected happened."

Hammett's description of what follows is a classic of brevity and lean prose:

> When I yanked Tai over backward by his fat throat, and slammed him to the floor, his guns were still barking metal; and they clicked empty

as I got a knee on one of his arms. I didn't take any chances. I worked on his throat until his eyes and tongue told me that he was out of things for a while. Then I looked around.

Thomas Quarre was against the bed, plainly dead, with three round holes in his starched white vest.

Across the room, Mrs. Quarre lay on her back. Her clothes had somehow settled in place around her fragile body, and death had given her once more the gentle friendly look she had worn when I first saw her.

"The House in Turk Street" reveals the young Hammett as a writer of his time in the casting of his villain as a sinister Oriental à la Fu Manchu (foreigners with exotic names and accents appear in a number of the early stories—"Dead Yellow Women" being an apotheosis of this trend), but his realism and straightforward prose set him apart. The story's epilogue is also pure Hammett. First the Op reads up on the gang in the newspaper (filling in all the information that would have come first in a standard detective yarn), then, during the next few days, turns up an even more fascinating tale: the *real* story behind the gang's activities. Once again we see Hammett fascinated with the idea of things being something other than what they seem. Behind the games are other, still more complicated games. Reality becomes a kind of onion.

The story ends, atypically, with an ellipsis—for the mysterious young woman has eluded the police dragnet. A loose end left hanging.

That loose end was to be picked up again in "The Girl with the Silver Eyes," published two months later, in the June issue of *Black Mask,* which had gone more or less monthly in the interim. The tale, however, is not told as a sequel to the earlier story. Its mysterious unfolding is far more cunning, one might even say playful.

It begins, by way of a lovely irony, with the Op taking on a "missing person" case. The person he has been hired to find is the fiancée of one Burke Pangburn, a pale poet-type who mopes about his apartment in wine-colored pajamas and a dressing gown covered with large jade-green parrots. Hammett's vivid characterization of this forlorn fellow, an odd mix of the tongue-in-cheek (naming him *Pangburn*) and the sympathetic, quickly seduces our credulity. He

seems too naive to be capable of deceit. Still, the ever-skeptical Op
sizes him up warily.

> The two great bugaboos of a reputable detective agency are the
> persons who bring in a crooked plan or a piece of divorce work all
> dressed up in the garb of a legitimate operation, and the irresponsible
> person who is laboring under wild and fanciful delusions—who wants a
> dream run out.
>   This poet—sitting opposite me now twining his long, white fingers
> nervously—was, I thought, sincere; but I wasn't so sure of his sanity.

Since the Op has already decided to take the case, this last
remark seems intended more as hard-boiled hyperbole than as a
serious judgment. It will turn out that the detective was right on
both counts: The woman is really missing, but his client is also a
"person laboring under wild and fanciful delusions." She is not who
he thinks she is, and she is not missing for the reasons he thinks.

The point here is that Pangburn's reality has got to be the Op's
starting point, and ours. It is all there is to go on. There are glimpses
of her in their letters, their reported conversations, but always in
the context of Pangburn's feelings, his sense of who she is. The
great lesson a detective learns—a lesson this story and almost all
of Hammett's, for that matter, reiterate—is that any one person's
reality is only a version of the truth, a subjective interpretation of
people and events based on what he has experienced, been told or
surmised, and on what he wants to believe. A detective is concerned
not only with ferreting out the truth, but with his own survival as
well. Cast adrift on a sea of unknowns, he must be skeptical not
only of everybody else's version of reality, but his own, too. Which
is why the Op is continually re-evaluating his sense of what is
happening.

But he is not a clairvoyant. There is no reason to assume, as he
pieces together his picture of the missing woman from her letters
and Pangburn's account, that she is somebody he already knows in a
different context. And it is an irony Hammett clearly enjoys pro-
longing. We are fully two-thirds of the way through the story before
the detective meets the missing lady and, her altered appearance
notwithstanding, is struck by a curious feeling of déjà vu. It is only
when she smiles—a familiar "mocking smile that bared the edges of

razor-sharp little animal-teeth," that he knows her, recognizing her not so much by a distinctive feature as by a characteristic little unguarded moment in which her face mirrors her soul. His own face ironically betrays the usually poker-faced Op in a similarly unguarded moment: "Recognition must have shown in my eyes in spite of the effort I made to keep them blank, for, swift as a snake, she had left the arm of the chair and was coming forward, her eyes . . ."—he savors the subtle observation even as the room is thrown into chaos with desperate characters diving for guns, cover and the light switch, plunging everything into darkness—". . . more steel than silver."

The swift action scenes that follow are among the most exciting Hammett had ever sketched. Indeed much of his charm as a writer lies in the fact that he combines a witty treatment of character and dialogue with a matchless skill at building scenes of action. Through it all his stocky hero moves with the singleminded and businesslike behavior of a professional getting down to work. He matter-of-factly applies the tricks of his trade Hammett had learned in the years with Pinkerton's—how to trace a piece of baggage or a canceled check, or looking up the weather conditions for a given period ("a trick that had worked well for me before") on the chance that someone would have been likely to take a cab and in so doing leave a record of a destination. Indeed Hammett admitted in a subsequent *Black Mask* letter to the editor that many of the story's details, including the character of the stoolie Porky Grout, were "based on things I've either run into personally or heard second hand from other detectives."

But while the ex-Pinkerton man has some fairly hard-boiled things to say about police informants or stool pigeons, both in the story ("I had no illusions about Porky") and in his subsequent letter, he is at pains to point out that Grout is not a simple character. His fellow criminals do not really understand him; even the seasoned Op admits he is taken totally by surprise by the stoolie's rather dramatic manner of dying. Porky's original, according to Hammett's letter, died in later years of tuberculosis. In inventing a final moment for him that is rather more "amazing" (the Op's word), Hammett seems to be answering a need in himself to go beyond the merely authentic into a deeper kind of truth about human beings. There is often more to them, he is saying, than meets the eye. And it is this that makes life—and detective stories—interesting.

A man cannot even be entirely sure of himself. Before this story is ended, the Op will undergo a terrifying moment of self-doubt—not on the business end of a loaded gun or at the point of a knife, but sitting in the front seat of a car, beside a beautiful woman. He is taking her in to stand trial. They have pulled over to the side of the road, at her request, and turned off the engine. In a scene that foreshadows the closing pages of *The Maltese Falcon*, in which Brigid O'Shaughnessy, caught red-handed, throws herself on Sam Spade's mercy, the Op's lovely prisoner blurts out her story. All very credible, familiar stuff. The way men and women get caught up with each other, entangled in little deceits that turn into bigger ones. Was she really so terrible—more criminal, finally, than victim? Her frightened, hurried appeal to the Op's humanity, then to his virility, prove unsettling.

> Her voice died, and she shivered a little. The robe I had given her had fallen away from her white shoulders. Whether or not it was because she was so close against my shoulder, I shivered, too. And my fingers, fumbling in my pocket for a cigarette, brought it out twisted and mashed.

She has gotten to him. He clears his throat, "struggling to keep my voice as casual as the words." His mouth is dry, but he fights down the impulse to moisten his lips. Desperate, hurt, knowing now that she faces jail and very likely the gallows, she makes one last rather touching appeal for "at least a hint that if I were not a prisoner your pulse might beat a little faster when I touch you. . . . Can't I take my vanity there not quite in tatters to keep me company? Can't you do some slight thing to keep me from the afterthought of having bleated all this out to a man who was simply bored?" She closes her eyes and moves closer to him. "You're beautiful as all hell!" the detective shouts "crazily into her face," flinging her against the door.

Thundering once again toward San Mateo County Jail, his foot to the floor, he squints through his bullet-shattered windshield "straight ahead into the wind that tore at my hair and face," so intent on his madly racing thoughts that he misses his turnoff and has to double back. It is not only that he is in a hurry to get her to San Mateo. Something else is at issue here. Feeling himself so close to losing control of his emotions, of his tough, protective persona, the Op needs to feel himself in command of a heavy vehicle hurtling all but out of control. "I let the car out another notch, *holding the road somehow*" (My italics).

Then, responding to what is evidently even a deeper need, and maybe the only cure, ultimately, for what ails him, he pulls over again to talk to her. "I knew I was shouting foolishly," he tells the reader, "but I was powerless to lower my voice." It is *his* version of the story—the version he believes—that he gives her now: her *real* motives, her *real* character.

The fact that he knew all of this or had surmised it all along and was still so deeply moved by her appeal says a lot about the Op's vulnerability and his humanity. The repeated references to his "rather lumpy profile" in the course of this scene—she addresses him as "little fat detective" no fewer than three times—are no accident. Elvira, for her part, is tenderly drawn—insincere, needful, sexy, frightened, not without some shreds of innocence. But his hero can feel all this, Hammett is saying, and still do his job. And that is what makes *him* interesting.

It has become clear with the second part of the young Hammett's most ambitious effort (24,000 words) to date that this writer is concerned with more than whodunit or hair-raising action scenes or hard-boiled posturing. "I turned on all the lights in the room, lighted a cigarette (we all like to pose a little now and then)," the Op had said back in "The House on Turk Street." At the end of "The Girl with the Silver Eyes," he confides that, "I didn't look at her, nor, I think, did she look at me, while she was being booked." Even in detective stories, says Hammett, endings are sometimes more complicated than beginnings.

But lest the reader wax sentimental, he has saved one more twist of the knife.

> As she was being led away, she stopped and asked if she might speak privately with me.
> We went together to a far corner of the room.
> She put her mouth close to my ear so that her breath was warm again

on my cheek, as it had been in the car, and whispered the vilest epithet of which the English language is capable.

Without this final glimpse of Elvira's true character, we might have been tempted to doubt the Op's fevered account of her cruelties, and to think him the crueler of the two in his rejection of her pitiable plea. In one stroke Hammett confirms everything the Op has thought about her and wrenches the reader back into the cold realities of his detective's world. To have trusted this woman, to have let go of his feelings even a little bit, might have proven a fatal misstep. A man less clear-eyed, less sure of himself and his methods, might have faltered. As might a man who took his job less seriously. Though the Op makes no closing comment of his own on what has taken place, letting her have the last word instead, Elvira's bitter gesture is finally less a comment on herself than on the man to whom she speaks. He is a man who takes his work very seriously.

3
The Poet of Violence:
Pain and Detachment in
Early Hammett

"He lay there, dead-still, except for a thin worm of blood
that crawled out of his hair to the rug."

"The Gutting of Couffignal" (1925)

If the four stories discussed thus far provide many fascinating
glimpses into the working habits of a real-life detective, "The
Whosis Kid," which appeared in *Black Mask* the following March
(1925), is a portrait of the Op as a company man. He has been
assigned to no case. He has chosen to shadow a suspicious character
known as "The Whosis Kid" strictly on his own initiative. He has
recognized him as a particularly vicious gunman once pointed out to
him by a fellow detective he had worked with before the war at the
Continental's Boston branch—a colleague named Lew Maher who
was killed by a "prowler" a few weeks later. Whether the Kid was
the "prowler" in question is never made clear.

Having the Op pursue the killer of a slain comrade in a classic
vendetta situation would have been irresistible to many a lesser
writer. But Hammett's hero betrays neither any particular emotion

over his colleague's death nor any stirrings of vengeance. When he thinks of Lew Maher at all it is only to recall the other man's warning about the Kid: "He can shoot and he's plain crazy. He ain't hampered by nothing like imagination or fear of consequences." Or as the Op himself later describes him, with his usual perspicuity: "His eyes were dead circles without any color you could name—the dull eyes of the man whose nerves quit functioning in the face of excitement"—just the worst sort of person to go up against.

But the same writer who deliberately short-circuited the potentially sentimental ending of "The Girl with the Silver Eyes" again passes over the obvious possibility—a tale of revenge—to give us a portrait of a nine-to-five detective who, whatever his own principles and private sense of honor, sees himself as an employe of the Continental Detective Agency. Consider the unabashed pragmatism of the Op's explanation of his decision to shadow the Kid:

> So far as I knew, the Whosis Kid wasn't wanted anywhere—not by the Continental, anyway—and if he had been a pickpocket, or a con man, or a member of any of the criminal trades in which we are only occasionally interested, I would have let him alone. But stick-ups are always in demand. The Continental's most important clients are insurance companies of one sort or another, and robbery policies make up a good percentage of the insurance business these days.

Soon finding himself closing in on what looks to be an imminent shoot-out between the Kid and some of his friends, he almost revels in his businesslike detachment. "My hope was that by hovering on the fringes until somebody won, I could pick up a little profit for the Continental, in the form of a wanted crook or two among the survivors." Here is neither mercenary bounty hunter nor crusading crime fighter, but a practical company man who gets satisfaction out of turning in a good day's work. "The idea in this detective business," he observes later, rejecting a dangerous move, "is to catch crooks, not to put on heroics."

At forty, the ever paunchy Op is clearly losing the battle of the bulge. With "twenty years" of this unpretty business behind him, he has begun to show traces of weariness as well as wisdom. "The day is past when I'll fight for the fun of it," he confides, "But I've been in too many rumpuses to mind them much." (In the ensuing tussle, the Op's description of his burly foe—marked by the world-weary lyricism of one who has seen it all—is nearly comic in its effect: "His fists were large as wastebaskets. They wheezed through the air." Though the struggle is earnest enough.) Later, surrounded by several vicious types with guns drawn—the very air trembling with imminent violence—his prose is a model of detachment ("It was a pretty tableau"). He describes each of the desperate characters almost lovingly, lastly himself—"not feeling so comfortable as I would home in bed, but not actually hysterical either."

Meanwhile he stalks his prey with professional calm. A nine-hour vigil in his parked car, with not so much as a glimpse of the subject and nothing to eat, as he likes to say, but cigarettes, displays not only the Op's profound patience but his seriousness and dedication to his job, his strong-willed determination and his ability to endure what sometimes seems an endless amount of discomfort uncomplainingly. He knows his way around police stations, what can and can't be done ("License plates, once they get started in crooked ways, are about as easy to trace as Liberty Bonds"), and what is counterproductive behavior (he gives a memo from the agency back to the messenger because "there's no wisdom in carrying around a pocketful of stuff relating to your job"). He is alert, always thinking, even during a tussle ("His other hand gouged at my face. That told me the bag was in the one I held"). He is observant, habitually registering basic descriptions of each new player who enters the game—always, as elsewhere in Hammett's stories—the kind of description a detective would like to get from a witness: detailed, clear, occasionally insightful (he recognizes the Whosis Kid from the back, from two rows behind him at a prize fight, seven years later and a continent away, by his distinctive ears—though the Op admits, wonderfully, "I didn't place them right away"). He grasps character quickly ("It was a stupid voice"), and he is, as always, wary of emotional involvement.

Finding himself in the sudden role of protector to a mysterious dark woman named Inés, he coolly sizes up the situation: "I didn't kid myself that my beauty and personality were responsible for any of her warmth. . . . She was in a jam. . . . I was something to be put between her and trouble." He reminds himself—shades of "The Girl with the Silver Eyes"—that "when the last gong rings I'm going to

be leading this baby and some of her playmates to the city prison. . . . an excellent reason—among a dozen others I could think
of—why I shouldn't get mushy with her." For all this, he confesses,
"I'd be a liar if I didn't admit she had me stirred up inside—between
her cuddling against me, giving me the come-on, and the brandy I
had drunk." For all his toughness and hard-boiled patter, Hammett's hero is a vulnerable man who feels, doubts, and, on occasion,
bleeds. What saves him is his ability to distinguish, most of the time,
between the sincere and the insincere ("Everything else about this
brown woman was all wrong, but her fright was real"), his dedication to his job, and his schooled detachment, which usually takes the
form of cynicism.

The familiar imagery of the poker game is here, too. He bluffs
("I had to look trusting and credulous. I expected to disbelieve
everything she said"), and conceals his real motives ("I had to
cover up my own game") while he tricks his opponents into reveal-
ing their hands (" 'Do your friends—the people you had your row
with tonight—know where you live?' I asked. I knew they did. I
wanted to see what she knew"). And every now and again he takes a
calculated risk and ups the ante ("I wondered—I took a chance.
'Aw, go jump down the sewer!' I told her"). In no other story found
in the two collections being considered here does one have a greater
sense of the Op's playing with his adversaries. Unlike the situation
in which he found himself on Turk Street, he has intruded into the
midst of this bunch of desperadoes by his own choice and with his
eyes open. He knows things about them that they don't realize he
knows, and, best of all, they do not know who he really is (he is
posing as a bootlegger) and what he is after. He feels his way into the
plot by deliberate if often spontaneous moves. "So far, so good. I
had started with the Whosis Kid, dropped him to take Maurois, and
now let him go to see who this woman was. I didn't know what this
confusion was all about, but I seemed to be learning *who* it was all
about."

The atmosphere of danger is, however, quite palpable, and the
many action scenes are thrillingly sketched—no cerebral armchair
detective story this one—including another even more spine-chilling
sequence in a pitch dark room, where the Op crouches waiting for
the Kid, who has already gotten into the apartment and knows he is

in there. In a flash of inspiration the detective has placed his watch across the room, on the theory that anyone coming through the door must, if only for a split second, pass in front of its phosphorescent dial. The suspense grows unbearable, as the Op's eyes begin to play tricks on him.

> The luminous patches on my watch burnt my eyes. I couldn't afford to blink. A foot could pass the dial while I was blinking. I couldn't afford to blink, but I had to blink. I blinked. I couldn't tell whether something had passed the watch or not. I had to blink again. Tried to hold my eyes stiffly opened. Failed. I almost shot at the third blink. I could have sworn something had gone between me and the watch. . . . My eyes smarted. Moisture filmed them. I blinked it away, losing sight of the watch for precious instants.

During this scene, and elsewhere in "The Whosis Kid," moments of violence particularly are described with Hammett's characteristic love of indirection, giving them an eerie quality. In "The Girl with the Silver Eyes" the Op described the unreal experience of being shot at by a man standing in the middle of the road while the detective races toward him in his black coupe: "The guns in his hands seemed to glow dimly red and then go dark in the glare of my headlights—glow and then go dark, like two bulbs in an automatic electric sign.

"The windshield fell apart around me."

In "The Whosis Kid," a black cadillac with curtained windows skids past a street corner where the Kid is walking—

> A curtain whipped loose in the rain.
> Out of the opening came pale fire-streaks. The bitter voice of a small-caliber pistol. Seven times.
> The Whosis Kid's wet hat floated off his head—a slow balloon-like rising.

This is wonderful writing, satisfying in its spareness as it is evocative in its indirection. It *shows,* in an almost cinematic way, rather than tells. It is also highly realistic. No one has ever seen a bullet *do* anything. Only the physical evidence of its presence—the flash, the noise of a gun, the alteration in or movement of what has been hit— are ever recorded by the human senses. The writer of these lines cannot have been unaware of the profound moral-distancing effect

of the separation of the often brilliant visual aspect of destruction
from a sense of the pain and ruin that accompany it. The last
sentence alone, with its image of the Kid's hat "floating" upward,
must place Dashiell Hammett high in the pantheon of the poets of
violence.

But for all the Op's detachment and vaunted pragmatism, the
reader is never quite allowed to think of him as an amoral type, as in
this scuffle that occurs late in the story:

> I twisted around, kicking the Frenchman's face. . . . Clawing fingers
> tore my mouth. I put my teeth in them and kept them there. One of my
> knees was on his face. I put my weight on it. My teeth still held his
> hand. . . .
> Not nice, this work, but effective.

It is, to be sure, a subtle point. But the fact that Hammett bothers to
add this closing comment at all is noteworthy. It has the effect of
acknowledging, at least indirectly, a moral perspective in a situation
in which no mention of such a thing would be highly understandable.
Anything goes, obviously, in a struggle of life and death, and the Op
is an accomplished street fighter; but in the larger game, he is
continually hinting, anything doesn't. One will search hard in these
stories to find Hammett's hero committing a gratuitous act of
violence, even upon the worst of men. And atrocities are atrocities.
There has to be some way, after all, to tell the good guys from the
bad guys—an axiom that has lost some favor with the post-James
Bond school of international crimefighting.

The Op's final summary of the case reveals a familiar pattern: a
man, in fact a series of men, exploited by a woman who has found
their weak points. But there is a deeper theme: that of trust—not
only between a man and woman, but as the very basis of society, the
sine qua non without which the social contract collapses. A jeweler's assistant named Binder trusted a woman (Inés); but for that
matter Binder was (in Hammett's words) "a trusted employee"—
"the faithful Binder." On the one hand, there was "the scheme *as
Binder knew it*. . . . Between Inés, Maurois and the Kid there was
another agreement" (italics mine). The classic double cross.
"Then," says the Op, "had come the sweet mess of quadruple and
sextuple crossing"—the whole series of private agreements between

Inés and each of her accomplices—"that had led all three into calamity. . . ." ("She twisted the pair of us, Frenchy, just like we twisted the boob," says the Kid. "Ain't you got it yet?")

Trust, Hammett's stories bring home repeatedly, *real* trust, is not possible except where there is an individual sense of honor. "Why cannot you trust me when you are with me?" this same Inés asks the Whosis Kid at one point in the Op's presence. "I tried to look trusting and credulous," the detective remarks of his own encounter with her on another occasion. "I expected to disbelieve everything she said." Where there can be no trust, assume none.

This issue of trust is perhaps the single most important theme in Hammett's work. It is found again and again at the heart of his stories and novels. To be sure, it is the basis of many a detective story, but with Hammett it is a theme that was to preoccupy him, in one way or another, to the end of his career. And if the betrayal of trust in his stories seems to occur more often between a man and a woman than between persons of the same sex, it probably has something to do with the greater vulnerability most men seem to feel in the presence of a charming woman, the susceptibility to flattery and self-delusion. The experience of women may be, if one is to believe the literature, similar, but Hammett's experience is after all that of a man.

"I won't pretend I trust you," his client's wife tells the Op in "The Main Death" (first published in June 1927). "There's only the two of us," he points out. "You can deny everything afterward. It's my word against yours. . . . Your one chance is to trust me." She is right to be leery. He has, he has told us, "concocted a wonderful series of lies to be told my client's wife—a series that I thought would get me the information I wanted." Before long we are into the classic poker game (" 'You're tying my hands,' I complained, standing up, pretending I wasn't watching her carefully.") Finally the bluff: He picks up the phone and asks for the detective bureau.

> Mrs. Gungen, standing in the sitting-room [sic], said, so softly I could barely hear it:
> "Wait."
> Holding the phone, I turned to look through the door at her. She was pinching her red mouth between thumb and finger, frowning. I didn't

> put down the phone until she took her hand from her mouth and held it
> out toward me. . . .
>   I was on top. I kept my mouth shut. It was up to her to make the
> plunge. She studied my face for a minute or more before she began:
>   "I won't pretend I trust you."

As it turns out, her trust is well placed. The Op solves the case
and recovers the missing money, but manages, through some fancy
footwork, to conceal her embarrassing secret. When she thanks
him, he "growls" a petulant acknowledgement, but the fact is his
sense of decency and compassion has won the day. No matter that
what he is concealing is her unfaithfulness. He has taken a distinct
dislike to his client, Bruno Gungen, whom he leaves with only the
minimal information he contracted to produce—Gungen "frothing at
the mouth, tearing his dyed goatee," a symbol of the fakery and
pretentiousness the Op cannot abide.

"His dinner jacket was corset-tight around his waist," he writes
on first meeting Gungen, "padded high and sharp at the shoulders.
Hair, moustache and spade-shaped goatee were dyed black and
greased until they were as shiny as his pointed pink fingernails. I
wouldn't bet a cent that the color in his fifty-year-old cheeks wasn't
rouge." His young wife's "painted mouth" and "general air of an
expensive doll in a toy-store window" are not in the same category.
Nor is her concealing something out of fearfulness, a motivation the
Op, as we have seen in other stories, can respect. At any rate she
eventually comes clean with him, while her habitually dishonest and
manipulative husband's behavior drives the Op to repeat the phrase
"dyed goatee" at least three times—even as he did with the dissembling Inés in "The Whosis Kid" ("It was what you would expect of a
woman who would dye her dog purple"). At the end of the story it
has the effect of justifying, at least in the Op's eyes, his decision to
suppress the whole truth.

Contrary to some of what has been written about Hammett's
detective, his cynicism is not absolute. He does have values beyond
doing his job well, and they play an important role in determining his
behavior.

But the truth to tell, though "The Main Death" is not without
its memorable touches ("she repeated the word mistress as if she
liked the shape of it in her mouth" and "he rolled his eyes in a

caricature of ecstasy"), it is probably the least compelling story in this collection—a living-room mystery that is closer to the cerebral whodunit of the classical English school than to the fast-moving, action-packed tale of the sort readers had come to expect from Hammett. It is interesting, though, for one other detail—its reference to the work of Hammett's contemporary Ernest Hemingway, with whom he has often been compared. When the Op meets Mrs. Gungen for the first time in the second floor sitting room she is reading a copy of *The Sun Also Rises*. In *Death in the Afternoon* (1932) Hemingway writes of how, while he was suffering from eye trouble, his wife would read aloud to him from "Dashiell Hammett's bloodiest to date, *The Dain Curse*." The many striking similarities between the Hemingway and Hammett styles—the edge of cynicism and spirit of disillusionment, the lean, tough sentences and realistic dialogue—have long been noted, even to the point of dubbing Hammett the Hemingway of detective fiction. And the question of who influenced whom has been debated almost as long.

The fact is that Hammett's first *Black Mask* tale appeared in 1922, the first Op stories the following year, long before the first collection of Hemingway's fiction, *In Our Time,* became available in this country in the fall of 1925, and then only in a limited edition. The stories had heretofore reached only limited audience in little magazines circulated on the Continent. By the time *The Sun Also Rises* appeared in the autumn of 1926, Hammett had published more than forty stories in various periodicals. (*Red Harvest* and *The Dain Curse* were the first Hammetts to reach hard covers, in 1929.) But Hemingway's revolutionary prose style was quite clearly formed between 1922 and 1923 in a garret in Paris, an ocean and a continent away from the bleak San Francisco hotel room where the young Dashiell Hammett, almost simultaneously, was finding his way into the style that was to revolutionize his own chosen genre. The most probable answer is that both men were children of the same post-war disillusionment and, through a unique chemistry of temperament and talent, were led to develop an approach to prose, character and action that most perfectly realized the alienated mood of the age in which they found themselves. No less a man of letters than André Gide, writing in the *New Republic* in 1944, compared "Dashiell Hammett's dialogues, in which every character is trying to deceive all the others and in which the truth slowly becomes visible through the haze of deception" with "the best in Hemingway." "The Main Death," alas, is probably not the most arresting example.

The final story in this collection, appropriately entitled "The Farewell Murder," is something else again. Published in *Black Mask* in February 1930, after the two Op novels, it is one of Hammett's soberest treatments of his fat, nameless detective. (He was to publish only one more Op tale, "Death and Company.") His reputation is established; he commands a higher fee than most other detectives, but he is known to be worth it. "Would I pay you what you are charging me, when I could get plenty of good enough detectives for half of that, if I did not require the best . . . ?" whines his client, a transplanted Russian nobleman named Kavalov (again foreigners provide an exotic element). Hammett even has Kavalov's son-in-law Ringgo remark aloud that he intends to stick around "to see how an expert handles these things." The fact is, Hammett is setting us up for a jolting turnabout.

Several pages into the story, the Op's client is murdered practically under his nose—a development all the more humiliating in that it has been made very clear that the Op was not brought to Kavalov's country estate to solve any crime at all—none had been committed yet—but to stop an old enemy from killing Kavalov as he had openly threatened to do. What makes it still worse is that the murder has been allowed to take place because of what the Op later admits was an error in judgment. "I had been wrong," he confesses, even as he takes pains to defend "my skill as a sleuth." The fact that Kavalov was a rather dislikable old sort makes his murder under these circumstances a bit easier to take than if he had been more sympathetic, but the Op is clearly on the spot and our confidence in him somewhat shaken.

Hammett wants it this way.

Our uneasiness is further fueled by the disconcerting sense that the tables have been turned on Hammett's gamester hero: Someone is playing—even toying—with him for a change. A scream and a body surprise him even before he has arrived at Kavalov's front door, the body as suddenly vanishes without a trace, and a murdered dog, a household pet, is soon after found roasting on a spit beside an abandoned campsite on the property. The Op is teased by a pair of brazen, almost maniacal jokesters who are the chief suspects. Then his frantic client is murdered, defiantly, his throat cut, while the detective sleeps under the same roof.

It is only his refusal to panic, to abandon his hard-won methods, his habit of cautiousness, his basically sensible approach to mystery, that sees the Op through. "I was tempted to get out of my coupé and do some snooping, but was afraid that I couldn't out-Indian Marcus on his own grounds," he says at one point. But if the old courage is there, too, it is never allowed to become hubris. "I knew the sort of folks I was playing with: I carried my gun in my hand." He pauses frequently "to think the situation over" or to "get it straight in my mind." He is good, but he is also human, and he knows it.

His secret weapon is that he knows other people are human, too, and does not forget it. As is his habit, the Op watches people's bodies closely for the little telltale signs of who they really are and how they really feel about things. Hammett knows that a person is all of a piece, that the body is—or becomes—the physical expression of a soul. "Kavalov raised a plump [read: self-indulgent] hand." "Sherry's eyes became hot grey points" as the Op tosses him an ambiguous answer. Even before the detective has met the members of Kavalov's family in the flesh we find him analyzing their voices coming from the next room, then matching them up with their owners as the people enter. And if, early on, he makes a bad error in judgment about who the real murderer is, it is because he has instinctively fastened on the most sinister one of the group, whose own peculiar pattern of treachery ultimately leads the detective to discover the truth.

The most interesting moment in the story occurs when the Op reveals his willingness to manipulate the truth—faking a confession from a dying man, to assure that justice will be done. "I've never been able to decide," he reflects afterward, telling us even more about his own personality and values,

> whether I would actually have gone on the witness stand and sworn that Sherry was alive when he nodded, and nodded voluntarily, if it had been necessary for me to do so to convict Ringgo.
>   I don't like perjury, but I knew Ringgo was guilty, and there I had him.

After all, in poker the idea of the "game"—an expression the Op uses three times in his summary of the case—is to win; whether you are actually holding all the cards your opponents think you are is irrelevant. "Fortunately," he notes, "I didn't have to decide," implying strongly that he would have committed perjury to convict a man he knew to be guilty. Interestingly enough, this situation allows the Op to remain a kind of idealist in the eyes of the reader, whereas if the story had actually concluded with an act of perjury, the reader's feelings about him might have been quite different. Even the hardened Op of the last stories does not dare to cross some lines of propriety.

Truly cynical behavior, he knows, is not forgiven: Of Kavalov's murderer, the Op says simply, "They hanged him."

4
Crooks and Capitalists: The Idealist Goes Armed

> "You have done this injury in the ordinary business manner—you understand?—for profit. There is not anything personal concerned."
>
> *Kavalov in "The Farewell Murder"*

"The Farewell Murder," which was reprinted in *Best American Mystery Stories of the Year* (Vol. I, 1931), is notable for another point it makes about Hammett's righteous sleuth: his not always too carefully hidden contempt for the rich. As one who finds himself frequently in their employ, the Op is deferential enough in his conversation and, ever the pragmatist, rarely critical of them to their faces. His asides are something else.

Hammett's most acerbic wit is reserved for the soulless capitalist who has amassed his fortune by exploiting others ruthlessly, putting aside human values, in the name of free enterprise or "the business ethic." Kavalov in "The Farewell Murder" epitomizes the type:

> "Supposing"—he wrinkled his forehead so that his bald scalp twitched forward—"you have done injury to a man ten years ago." He turned his wrists quickly, laying his hands palm-up on the white cloth. "You

have done this injury in the ordinary business manner—you understand?—for profit. There is not anything personal concerned. You do not hardly know him."

Hammett's only comment here is indirect, restricted to a couple of "stage directions" slipped into the pauses in Kavalov's little speech, which slyly evoke the contradictory imagery of the old man's guilt ("his bald scalp *twitched* forward") and would-be innocence ("laying his hands *palm-up* on the *white cloth*") [italics mine]. Note that both are conveyed in physical gestures. But the word *twitched,* in keeping with Hammett's understanding of body language, is meant to suggest an involuntary gesture, the imagery of the second aside a calculated (i.e., suspect) one. It is ironically Kavalov's own emphasis on the impersonal character of his own earlier dealings—to him a kind of value that preempts merely human considerations—that makes him contemptible in the Op's eyes, and ours. When the self-confessed cutthroat "businessman" has his own throat literally cut, we may be surprised, even shocked, but on another level we feel he had it coming.

The notion that wealth accumulated ruthlessly invites judgment is developed even more explicitly in several of the stories in *The Big Knockover*, a collection of some of Hammett's best short fiction ranging from the very first tale published under his real name, "The Gatewood Caper" of October 1923, to "Fly Paper," which appeared in August 1929, on the eve of the Crash. The Op's client in that very early tale, a lumber magnate named Harvey Gatewood, "had made his several millions," Hammett tells us, "by sandbagging everybody that stood in his way. . . ." He is an arrogant, thoroughly unpleasant man, and the proud detective comes within a hair of refusing to work for him.

Gatewood has received a ransom note demanding $50,000 for the return of his missing eighteen-year-old daughter Audrey. The writer of the note clearly finds the irony of the situation delicious: He is in possession of a commodity Gatewood clearly wants and can ask, cynically, whatever price the market will bear. "We have your charming daughter and place a value of $50,000 upon her," he begins, and concludes in a curt postscript: "We know someone who will buy her even after we are through with her—in case you won't listen to reason." The old capitalist is galled by this turnabout. He is damned, he says, if he will be "held up by anybody." It is only with great difficulty that the detectives manage to get him to put his daughter's safety ahead of his obsession with "his own fighting spirit."

When it turns out to be Audrey herself who has perpetrated the fake kidnapping for the purpose of gaining financial independence from her bullying father, the Op actually laughs out loud at what he cynically refers to as "a fine joke," calling her "a chip off the old block."

> Remembering some of the business methods Harvey Gatewood had used—particularly some of his war contracts that the Department of Justice was still investigating—I suppose the worst that could be said about Audrey was that she was her father's own daughter.

A clear case of poetic justice. This heartless, hard-nosed business-man has produced an equally heartless, hard-nosed daughter, and she has very nearly beat him at his own game. At the beginning of the story, when the Op arrives on the scene, Gatewood is ranting about calling "these people's bluff!" On his way out, the Op observes, returning to the same poker imagery, that

> The card she beat him with was a threat of spilling everything she knew about him to the newspapers, and at least one of the San Francisco papers had been trying to get his scalp for years.
> I don't know what she had on him, and I don't think he was any too sure himself.

Practically all the hallmarks of Hammett's distinctive style are already visible in this early tale, which ran in *Black Mask* originally under the title of "Crooked Souls": the use of authentic police methods, the vivid action scenes, the hard-bitten, realistic dialogue, the gamester imagery. The Op is already a seasoned professional who recognizes a con man "who had been active in the east four or five years before" and "learned years ago to stand to one side of strange doors when making uninvited calls." He is overweight and cynical, poker-faced, and not without compassion. "I didn't like him either personally or by reputation," he remarks of Gatewood, ". . . but this morning I felt sorry for him."

The pedestrian ending ("I was glad it was over. It had been a tough caper") is a disappointment. The interesting thing here is that the Op can walk away almost indifferently from a closed case knowing that probably nobody—except maybe Gatewood himself—will ever be convicted. He does not permit himself even the smallest expression of bitterness. He seems content to enjoy the irony of the situation, and to take quiet satisfaction in the performance of his job. "I'm a detective," he explains in "The Gutting of Couffignal," the story that opens the *Knockover* volume, "because I happen to like the work . . . . And liking work makes you want to do it as well as you can. Otherwise there'd be no sense to it. . . . I don't know anything else, don't enjoy anything else, don't want to know or enjoy anything else," he tells his prisoner, who has just tried to buy him off with a bribe. "You can't weigh that against any sum of money."

Nor is it a prerequisite that he respect the people who hire him. To the reader at least the Op makes no secret of his contempt for the island's well-heeled citizens, most of whom are "well-fed old gentlemen who, the profits they took from the world with both hands in their younger days now stowed away at safe percentages, have bought into the island colony"—a fictional body of land supposed to be about two hours from San Francisco—"so they may spend what is left of their lives nursing their livers and improving their golf among their kind.

"They admit to the island," he tells us, "only as many storekeepers, working people, and similar riffraff as are needed to keep them comfortably served." The Op has been hired—by the owners, he hastens to point out, of Couffignal's largest house—to guard the wedding presents at a nuptial gala of international proportions. VIPs and foreign nobility, both employed and out-of-work, are everywhere (a curious combination of the twenties pulp penchant for exotic foreign villains and Hammett's prosaic real-life job experience with the Pinkerton agency, where he was once hired by a woman to discharge her housekeeper). Resigned to carrying out his dull assignment, the Op is counting the hours until he can take the ferry back to the mainland when the rainy night is disturbed by sounds of many rifle shots, machine-gun fire, explosions and the rushing footsteps of excited men. Couffignal is under seige: a mass looting is in progress.

The identity of the "invaders" is no haphazard detail. A band of exiled Russian aristocrats, deprived of property, privilege and capital by the Revolution (which in 1926, when the story appeared, was still fresh in the popular mind), are the culprits. Bitter and wearied of scraping out a meager existence "teaching music and languages, and so on," they have decided to take back from the world what was theirs by birth. The plundered are robbing the plunderers.

Judgment Day.

"The Gutting of Couffignal" is, on one level, a little parody of dog-eat-dog capitalism, even down to the investment of capital in this brash adventure. Having picked out Couffignal, one of the band later tells the Op, the conspirators leased a house for six months, "having just enough capital remaining to do that and to live properly here while our plans matured."

Interestingly enough, the Op makes no comment on this obvious irony, either to the reader or to the ringleader of the marauding band in the course of their eventual confrontation. The point has been made, as in the case of Kavalov, by the actors themselves. Instead the detective addresses himself—in what amounts to almost an extended tirade—to another issue. He challenges the ringleader's statement that the plot failed as part of a general pattern of doom that seems to be the group's lot, and that in the Op they ran up against some kind of "genius." The hard truth, he says, is that it was their own incompetence (a quality he disdains even in criminals) that brought about their defeat. He uses the word "amateur" more than once to describe their behavior, which he contrasts contemptuously with the behavior of "professional" criminals. Their mistake, he implies, was in viewing their adventure as a holy cause that had the force of divine justice behind it rather than as a piece of cold business, a *job* to be accomplished—"The truth is you people botched your job from beginning to end"—while he, as a trained professional, took precisely that approach.

The tale is a study of the Op's own competence. From almost the moment chaos descends on the island, he calmly takes charge, directing his forces this way and that in the night like a stand-in general, continually sizing up what begins as an utterly baffling situation, searching out the strong points and weaknesses of his foe. With panic and treachery all around him, he proceeds with his old deliberateness and an economy of action, awaiting his opening, the one moment in which his own limited resources can have their optimum effect.

> Rolling into the hedge, I lay there, straining my eyes through the spaces between the stems. I had six bullets in a gun that hadn't yet been fired on this night that had seen tons of powder burned.
> When I saw wheels on the lighter face of the road, I emptied my gun, holding it low. . . .
> There was a grinding sound. A crash. The noise of metal folding on itself. The tinkle of glass.
> I raced toward those sounds.

But if the Op likes to view his own forward progress as a series of decisions ("I . . . had just decided to bite it"—referring to his assailant's gun arm), there is always the element of the unpredictable to contend with, and his own occasional lapses of grace. "I clicked my gun at him, forgetting I had emptied it." "A stone, turning under my foot, threw me sidewise, twisting my ankle." "I hadn't thought of that."

When a gunman, coming up behind him unnoticed, gets the drop on him, the Op curses himself for having been "too careless, or too vain, to keep a gun in my hand while I talked to the girl." The reference to his vanity relates back to the Op's old vulnerability: he knows that he has certain weaknesses and does not entirely trust himself in certain situations. When he launches into his tirade about the band's amateurism and his own love affair with his work, it is because his antagonist—who has been "studying me with mournful large eyes that made me feel like fidgeting"—has made him uncomfortable. "You think I'm a man and you're a woman," he concludes brusquely, adjusting his borrowed crutch, "That's wrong. I'm a manhunter and you're something that has been running in front of me. There's nothing human about it."

The point is, of course, that the Op is only too painfully aware of his humanity and his compassionate instincts. His little soapbox speech about his work begins with the words, "We'll disregard whatever honesty I happen to have, sense of loyalty to employers, and so on." Though he prefers to explain his integrity in more down-to-earth, purely pragmatic terms—because, he says, she "might doubt" the more altruistic ones—the fact that the Op takes the time to mention them at all shows his (and Hammett's) preoccupation with higher values. And when—in yet one more rehearsal for the famous Brigid O'Shaughnessy/Sam Spade confrontation—he puts a bullet in her leg as she tries to leave, he is deeply troubled. In fact, his sense of who he is is severely shaken. "You ought to have known I'd do it!" he yells angrily ("My voice sounded harsh and savage and like a stranger's in my ears"), quickly covering his vulnerability in the very next breath with a piece of mock self-deprecation that is pure cynical slapstick: "Didn't I steal a crutch from a cripple?"

The Op's anxiety about what is happening to his humanity is further revealed in his presentation of his superior at the Continental's San Francisco office, an enigmatic character known only as the Old Man. Conversations with his boss figure in both of the stories that follow "Couffignal" in the *Knockover* collection.

In "Fly Paper," the Old Man receives the news that a pretty young woman has been found dead with an unruffled "Indeed"— "as if," notes the Op, "I had said it was raining." In "The Scorched Face" (originally published some four years earlier, in May 1925), the Op tells us of "his gentle eyes behind gold spectacles and his mild smile, hiding the fact that fifty years of sleuthing had left him without any feelings at all on any subject." If the Old Man is a living lesson to the younger detective that people are not always what they seem, he is also a disturbing reminder of what can happen to a man who spends too many years of his life dealing with treachery and deceit: the psychological equivalent of what happens to rock musicians and other manual laborers. The calluses they develop could be described as a kind of protective scar tissue that prevents them from feeling routinely encountered pain that would otherwise get in the way of their work. The Old Man is described even more vividly in "The Big Knockover," written two years later, as a "tall, plump man in his seventies . . . with a white-mustached, baby-pink, grandfatherly face"—the narrator/Op plays the incongruity of the benevolent exterior for all it is worth—"mild blue eyes behind rimless spectacles, and no more warmth than a hangman's rope." The contrast is clearly meant to be unsettling. Even sinister.

> Fifty years of crook-hunting for the Continental had emptied him of everything except brains and a soft-spoken, gentle smiling shell of politeness that was the same whether things went good or bad—and meant as little at one time as another. We who worked under him were

proud of his cold-bloodedness. We used to boast that he could spit
icicles in July, and we called him Pontius Pilate among ourselves,
because he smiled politely when he sent us out to be crucified on
suicidal jobs.

The admiration is sincere. But just as real is the Op's recurring
anxiety that he too will end up feeling nothing, permanently cut off
from his own body's truth as well as from contact with other human
beings—an emotional and moral zombie. "I've got horny skin all
over what's left of my soul," he notes touchingly only a few pages
later, hearing the pathetic cry of a dying man, "but just the same my
forehead twitched. The scream was so damned weak for what it
said," adds a man who still knows—feels—that a man going into
eternity at the hands of another man is a monstrous thing, or as
Raymond Chandler would later put it in a reflection on Hammett's
work, "an act of infinite cruelty." It is not without significance that
nearly every time the Op mentions his callousness, it is coupled with
an instance of some intense feeling that he seems almost surprised to
learn survives in him.

By the same token, he seems unable to acknowledge his feelings and nobler impulses (as in the speech about his work) except in
the safe context of some cynical or pragmatic patter. The Old Man is
merely calloused. The Op is cynical, almost militantly so. His hard-
boiled wisecracks betray a closet idealist. He has not yet let go of his
humanity. In "The Scorched Face" his compassion for "a lot of
families" leads him to destroy evidence and, even more dramati-
cally than we have seen before, suppress a part of the truth. He
pleads with a fellow detective to conspire with him in this act of
mercy ("I had come a lot nearer to being eloquent than ever before
in my life") and endures his colleague's abuse with great humility.
The Op's unselfish gesture is oddly undercut by a series of hints that
he is cynically manipulating the other man, then deepened by a
sudden revelation: it is the other detective himself, and his own
fragile young family, that the Op is trying to shield from a devastat-
ing discovery.

Hammett's moralistic orientation is reflected in the basic situations of "The Scorched Face" and the story that precedes it, "Fly
Paper," both of which turn on his old theme of wealth and corruption and the bitter price that it inevitably, sooner or later, exacts.

Both stories are set solidly in the milieu of the roaring twenties, a period rife with decadence and self-indulgence. In both, the well-bred daughters of affluent, socially prominent families have fled their pampered, empty lives in search of the exotic, of fun, of connection with something live and real. In "Fly Paper" it is the racy world of tough-talking gangsters and speakeasies—wonderfully evoked by Hammett's prose at its hard-boiled best and dialogue so thick with underworld argot and the hip jargon of the era that the reader practically needs a glossary. "The Scorched Face" describes a very different kind of Twenties thrill-seeking—the somewhat lesser known phenomenon of the quasi-religious cult, which parlayed the power of sexuality, repressed or unleashed, into an experience of ecstasy.

The murders in both stories eventually lead to what can only be described as rather exotic—which is not to say unbelievable—solutions. But they are arrived at very differently. "The Scorched Face" (the title refers to a charred photograph) follows the mystery step by careful step through the most relentless (and authentic) kind of police work to the sordid scene, finally, of the crime itself: the final problem is to figure out not what happened, but what to do about it. "Fly Paper" begins as an open-and-shut case—the only seeming problem being the apprehension of the killer—and proceeds, as various bizarre facts come to light, through a series of (continually revised) hypotheses until one is found that explains everything. The Old Man serves an additional function here. He is at once a teasing foil to the Op's own mental processes, and the fact that the younger detective is not intimidated by his superior's greater experience tells us something about the Op's respect for himself. He trusts his instincts, even when they appear foolish:

> "And what do you make of it?"
> I squirmed in my chair and said, "Suicide."
> The Old Man smiled at me, politely but skeptically.
> "I don't like it either," I grumbled. "And I'm not ready to write it in a report yet. But that's the only total that what we've got will add up to."

The real solution will prove to be somewhat more complicated than that, but he will turn out to have been very much on the right track.

The missing piece of the puzzle is found in the pages of a book discovered stashed in the victim's kitchen, a book that is probably not much read these days, at least by adults, but which fueled the imagination of many of those writers and artists who grew up to create the stuff of the pulp magazines and comic books of the Twenties and Thirties—from Jerry Siegel and Joe Shuster, the Cleveland high-school seniors who in 1934 created Superman, to Dashiell Hammett: *The Count of Monte Cristo*. Alexandre Dumas's 1844 swashbuckling tale, along with Dumas's immortal *The Three Musketeers* and *The Man in the Iron Mask*, may well have had a greater impact on that school of fiction than the (today) more highly regarded work of Arthur Conan Doyle. Even Hammett, who was already widely regarded as a champion of the new realism, occasionally confesses his fondness for the great nineteenth-century adventure yarns. If Mrs. Gungen in "The Gutting of Couffignal" prefers to curl up with Hemingway's latest, the Op himself is just as likely to while away the midnight hours on a boring job with something along the lines of *The Lord of the Sea*, which recounts the fictional adventures, he tells us, of "a strong, tough and violent fellow named Hogarth, whose modest plan was to hold the world in one hand. There were plots and counterplots, kidnapings, murders, prison-breakings, forgeries and burglaries, diamonds large as hats and floating forts larger than Couffignal. It sounds dizzy here," the Op admits, "but in the book it was as real as a dime."

The next three stories in *The Big Knockover* (excluding "The Gatewood Caper," which has already been discussed) offer evidence that Hammett, had he been so inclined, could have swashed bucklers with the best of them. All three forsake the familiar back streets of Hammett's San Francisco for exotic settings—a tiny (mythical) Balkan country in the throes of revolution ("This King Business"); the wild and woolly west ("Corkscrew"); and the sinister world-within-a-world of San Francisco's Chinatown ("Dead Yellow Women"). All three sport casts of characters that would have kept the Scarlet Pimpernel on his toes, let alone a middle-aged, overweight detective.

In each the Op's by now habitual role as the outsider, the one who is not in on the secret, is heightened by the unfamiliarity of his surroundings; the sense that he is really on his own, cut off from help; the sense in each case of a closed society with an elaborate set of rules and values all its own into which he has intruded; and in two of the stories the fact that his antagonists, at crucial moments, speak in a language that he does not understand. That Hammett manages most of the time to make it all "as real as a dime" is testimony not only to his vivid powers of invention and his engaging way with character, but also to his innate sense of restraint: nowhere is he tempted by the romantic nature of his materials to step, as the writer of Hammett's obituary in the *New York Times* said of him, beyond the boundaries of the credible.

"This King Business," which appeared in a magazine called *Mystery Stories* in January 1928, might easily have crossed the line. It concerns the young heir of an American fortune named Lionel Grantham who has set out with his millions to become king of a newly created country, the "youngest and smallest of the Balkan States" set up in the years following World War One as part of a newly reorganized Europe. Hammett undercuts what could have become an exercise of high camp almost from the start by putting the whole thing in the familiar context of money, corruption, and good old American spoiled affluence. "Seven months ago, on his twenty-first birthday," Muravia's U. S. charge d'affaires Roy Scanlan tells the Op:

> this Lionel Grantham got hold of the money his father had left him—a nice wad. Till then the boy had had a tough time of it. His mother had, and has, highly developed middle-class notions of refinement. His father had been a genuine aristocrat in the old manner—a hard-souled, soft-spoken individual who got what he wanted by simply taking it . . . the Grantham blood was the best in America.

The Op has been retained to track down the impetuous young Lionel and his $3 million and find out what he is up to "on the quiet" by the lad's uncle, Senator Walbourn. (The rich and the socially prominent are led to detective agencies rather than to the regular authorities in Hammett's stories, typically, out of their concern for reputation and the maintenance of a social order that depends at least partially on the suppression of truth. The facts they are trying to hush up—the misadventures of some relative—are usually directly traceable to the family's wealth and the darker side of affluence.) What Lionel is up to, it turns out, is backing a "peaceful" coup—in return for which selfless gesture the conspirators have decided to name him king of the small, impoverished country. This, Lionel reasons happily, would pave the way for a badly needed influx of American capital. It has the additional charm, he confides to the Op, of restoring a crown to the Grantham line, which traces its pedigree back to James IV of Scotland. The detective coolly agrees to help young Lionel through a steadily thickening plot of palace intrigue and thinly cloaked treachery "with a clean face"—"as if steering millionaire descendants of Scotch kings through Balkan plots were an old story to me, merely part of the day's work." Which, of course, is exactly how he approaches his task.

It is politics played as poker. "Each of us . . . was weighing the other before he said it." "I cursed myself for overplaying my hand. There was nothing to do now but spread the cards." Colonel Einarson, the chief conspirator, proves a wilier foe. The stakes, as always, are survival. "So while he talked I studied him, combing him over for weak spots. . . . I didn't know whether he had guts or not, but before an audience I guessed he'd make a grand showing, and most of this act would be before an audience. Off in a dark corner I had an idea he would go watery." Often unable to understand what is being said, the detective leans more heavily than ever on his skill in reading faces to uncover the dynamics of this little cast of characters:

> Einarson raised his hand, bawled a dozen words, growled at Djuda-kovich [the huge minister of police], and stepped back.
> Djudakovich spoke, a drowsy, effortless roar that could have been heard as far as the hotel. As he spoke he took a paper out of his pocket and held it before him. There was nothing theatrical in his voice or manner. He might have been talking about anything not too important. But—looking at his audience, you'd have known it was important.
> The soldiers had broken ranks to crowd nearer, faces were redden-ing, a bayoneted gun was shaken aloft here and there. Behind them the citizens were looking at one another with frightened faces.

One after another, the Op makes his guesses—what is written on the piece of paper, which of these bitter rivals will have the loyalty of the army—and takes his calculated gambles.

But even as he cynically manipulates the other players and

makes young Lionel (literally) king for a day—Lionel the Once, he calls him—the hardened detective finds himself at several points giving expression to the most unabashed romantic sentiments. "We can die," says Lionel Grantham gently, when it looks as though the revolution has gone against them. The Op opines:

> There wasn't the least bit of sense to that crack. Nobody was here to die. They were all here because it was so unlikely that anybody would have to die, except perhaps a few of Einarson's soldiers. That's the sensible view of the boy's speech. But it's God's own truth that even I—a middle-aged detective who had forgotten what it was like to believe in fairies—felt suddenly warm inside my wet clothes. And if anybody had said to me, "This boy is a real king," I wouldn't have argued the point.

Later he will confess himself "half sorry" the idealistic Lionel cannot remain behind as monarch.

This is the same Op who earlier felt moved to tell the reader he admired the efficient, "workmanlike manner" with which Einarson scourged a double-crossing soldier, and who can return to America content that he has left the little nation in the able hands of an unimaginative bureaucrat with "a digestion instead of a brain," whose occasional strong-arm tactics are at least offset by his lack of personal ambition. Thus does Hammett manage to keep his tale both unsentimental and credible. He is nowhere cynical about the idea of a revolution, but he is also realistic about political factions, ambitious men and the needs of government.

The aging scientist-scholar who had been honored with his country's presidency is forced to step down. Dr. Semich is a benign but ineffectual figure who never appears in the story. A world-renowned bacteriologist, he has been known to confide to intimate friends that he doesn't believe in the value of bacteriology at all. " 'Mankind must learn to live with bacteria as friends,' he'll say. 'Our bodies must adapt themselves to diseases, so there will be little difference between having tuberculosis, for example, or not having it. That way lies victory. This making war on bacteria is a futile business. Futile but interesting. So we do it. Our poking around in laboratories is perfectly useless—but it amuses us.' "

To Hammett, who had suffered nearly ten years from debilitat-

ing tuberculosis, beginning his writing career in what he believed to
be the shadow of his own imminent death and forced to live apart
from his family, this "delightful old dreamer" clearly had to go. The
sober business of holding a country together and keeping order was
better entrusted to more practical hands. When young Lionel,
caught up in the spirit of his new office, starts talking about staying
behind as king to do his best for the Muravians, who "have trusted
me," the Op pops his balloon unceremoniously: "My God, that's
old Doc Semich's line! . . . I made you king, understand? I made you
king so you could go home with your chin up—not so you could stay
here and make an ass of yourself!" It was Semich's naivete, we are
reminded, that precipitated the revolution.

Still, the odd thing here is that Hammett decided to insert—and
presumably thought up—Semich's charming theory in the first
place. Having once apparently despaired of ever being cured of
tuberculosis by then known medical treatments, Hammett had holed
up in a room by himself to write and live on soup, only to discover a
gradual remission of his symptoms. Is his little joke about bacteria
aimed less perhaps at the dreamers than at that other sort of
romantic who thinks an absolute solution to the problems of the
world is always just around the corner? The Op has no illusions
about the futility of his own fight against crime and injustice (for
which the leftist papers in fact censured Hammett). He is a detective
because, as Dr. Semich would say, it "amuses" him. But also, to
give him his due, because of his fierce sense of fair play. The Op is
sickened by the memory of his foe being literally torn apart by a
crowd of angered Muravians. "No matter how wrong a man is, if a
mob's against him, I'm for him," he tells Romaine Frankl, the
secretary of the minister of police. "The only thing I ever pray to
God for is a chance some day to squat down behind a machine gun
with a lynching party in front of me."

5
A Moll Named Grace:
The Search for Wholeness

"Do not become jealous of Jerry. Jerry is enamored of one yellow and white lady somewhere, and to her he is most faithful. Not even the smallest liking has he for dark women." She smiled a challenge at me. "Is it not so, Jerry?"
"No," I denied. "And, besides, all women are dark."

"The Whosis Kid"

The lovely, darkly mysterious secretary, Romaine Frankl, is only the latest incarnation of the character that appears with slight variations in so many of Hammett's stories: Inés, Jeanne Delano/ Elvira, Mrs. Gungen, Princess Zhukovski in "The Gutting of Couffignal," and, later, Dinah Brand in *Red Harvest*, Gabrielle Leggett in *The Dain Curse,* and—her apotheosis—Brigid O'Shaughnessy in *The Maltese Falcon*. A maddening blend of innocence and manipulation, vulnerability and villainy, sometimes she gets to him and sometimes the Op manages to keep her fixed in his cold eye. At times he gets downright playful.

He knows enough to be afraid of her, but always finds her intriguing (in the earlier stories she is frequently a foreign lady with a distinctly alien quality about her), and usually is soon in an uneasy alliance with her. In an atmosphere heavy with danger and malevolence, they do a dance of trust and manipulation.

I told her what I knew. When I had finished she pulled my head down to kiss me, and held it down to whisper, "You do trust me, don't you dear?"

"Yeah. Just as much as you trust me."

"That's far from being enough," she said, pushing my face away.

Marya came in with a tray of food. We pulled the table around in front of the divan and ate.

"I don't quite understand you," Romaine said over a stalk of asparagus. "If you don't trust me why do you tell me things? As far as I know, you haven't done much lying to me. Why should you tell me the truth if you've no faith in me?"

"My susceptible nature," I explained.

Of course the Op's Dark Lady doesn't always turn out to be a villainess. Romaine Frankl gets off with being pronounced "a cold-blooded hussy," and the reader is subtly informed by the Op's use of the word "us" in the final railroad station scene that she has decided after all to come back to San Francisco with him.

Of Romaine Frankl we hear no more. But she reappears as the enchanting young Chinese-American woman Lillian Shan in "Dead Yellow Women."

"She was sitting straight and stiff in one of the Old Man's chairs when he called me into the office—a tall girl of perhaps twenty-four, broad-shouldered, deep-bosomed, in mannish gray clothes," begins that story (originally published in November 1925). The daughter of a Manchu who had escaped to California with her and his millions ("presumably the accumulated profits of a lifetime of provincial misrule") when the Manchus had been driven from power in 1911, she has been educated at the finest eastern schools, acquiring several degrees, become proficient enough at tennis to have won some sort of trophy, and authored a book on the arcane subject of fetishes. This fascinating young woman more recently has also found herself caught up in the web of murder and intrigue that will take the Op into the spooky world of San Francisco's Chinatown.

The story's opening pages present a by-now familiar picture of the Op in his element. He is a man who knows the city and its denizens. This is his turf. He moves comfortably among the fringes of the underworld and is on first-name terms with a seemingly endless assortment of informers, small-time con men and other unsavory characters. Even in Chinatown, an area of only a dozen blocks adjacent to the Latin Quarter, the Op is "too well known," he fears, to do his own snooping around. It is the Chinatown on the other side of the locked doors that is an unknown world—a nightmare of tunnels connecting one house to another blocks away, a labyrinthine maze of trap doors and interconnected rooms, leaving the impression of whole houses within houses, from which desperate characters are liable to emerge at the drop of a pin.

With vivid, staccato prose Hammett evokes an almost visceral sense of lurking menace, the oppressive presence of violent men cooped up in a narrow space, stumbling over one another in dark passageways, men who move, dress and act with a strangeness that is unsettling.

> My guide spun around, twisting out of one slipper. In each of his hands was an automatic as big as a coal scuttle. Even while trying to get my own gun out I wondered how so puny a man could have concealed so much machinery on him.
>
> The big guns in the little man's hands flamed at me. Chinese-fashion, he was emptying them—crash! crash! crash! . . . His slugs shredded the wood as if it had been paper. His guns clicked empty.
>
> The door swung open, pushed by a wreck of a man who was trying to hold himself up by clinging to the sliding panel in the door's center.
>
> Dummy Uhl—all the middle of him gone—slid down to the floor and made more of a puddle than a pile there.
>
> The hall filled with yellow men, black guns sticking out like briars in a blackberry patch.

And the Op has only just arrived.

This passage also illustrates how Hammett keeps it all down to earth with his wonderfully fresh and playful similes (an automatic "as big as a coal scuttle," guns "sticking out like briars in a blackberry patch") and his deliberate use of inappropriate synonyms ("so much machinery"). A phrase like "all the middle of him gone"—so startlingly vivid that it catches at our stomachs involuntarily—is immediately juxtaposed with the cartoon-grotesque image of a man dissolving into a puddle. A scene of heart-stopping terror has been recreated by a man with a rather engaging sense of humor. "You give 'em," says his Chinese guide, reaching to take the detective's gun, which has never gotten off a shot. "I gave 'em," the Op tells the reader, and adds: "He could have had my pants."

The Op's sense of humor is also displayed in his encounters with a kind of elderly Chinese godfather figure named Chang Li Ching, his inscrutable host, who continually pulls the detective's leg by playing an exaggerated version of Confucius in high drag. ("Did death honor our hovel yesterday?") Chang mischievously addresses the Op, in mock oriental politeness, with titles like "Father of Detectives," "Terror of Evildoers," "King of Finders-Out," "Master of Mysteries," and "Grandfather of Bloodhounds." The Op can play this game, too.

> "I beaned one of your servants last night," I said when he had run out of flowers for the time. "I know there's nothing I can do to square myself for such a terrible act, but I hope you'll let me cut my throat and bleed to death in one of your garbage cans as a sort of apology."

Though the Op complains to the reader about all the "nonsense" he is being subjected to at the hands of Chang, he clearly enjoys the old man, who is, he finally admits, that rara avis, an interesting foe. "I liked him. He had humor, brains, nerve, everything. To jam him in a cell would be a trick you'd want to write home about. He was my idea of a man worth working against."

But "Dead Yellow Women" never becomes, as it might have, a mere duel of two champions of good and evil in an exotic setting. Hammett is always Hammett, and sticks to what he knows, what obsesses him. All of these wildly fanciful elements lead right back to the old realities of prohibition America and a familiar situation—the black-sheep son of a wealthy and prominent family up to his ears in trouble—and to the mysterious woman who has won the Op's sympathy but, as in her other incarnations, has not trusted him enough to have told him everything.

> Boiling like a coffeepot before we were five miles out of Filmer, the automobile stage carried me south into the shimmering heat and bitter white dust of the Arizona desert.

The wonderful cinematic image with which the story "Corkscrew" opens transports us with one stroke into what was left in September 1925 of America's wild west. The ornery little cowtown of Corkscrew, nestled among the dust-cracked arroyos and parched mesas just north of the Mexican border, is for practical purposes the last outpost of anarchy on a long-since civilized frontier.

"Ladiesh an' gentsh," intones a drunk solemnly as the Continental Op signs in at the hotel on the back of an envelope the desk clerk has slid over to him, "th' time hash came for yuh t' give up y'r evil ways an' git out y'r knittin'. Th' law hash came to Orilla County!"

Black Mask's readers were probably a lot less startled than Hammett's present-day readers to find their favorite private eye in this improbable setting. The magazine, like other pulps, routinely featured action-charged sagebrush sagas as part of its fare, along with love stories and tales of the occult. Hammett's fellow regular contributor, Erle Stanley Gardner, now remembered as the creator of the indomitable defense attorney Perry Mason, ground out, among other things, several ongoing western series starring such intrepid hombres as Bob Larkin, Black Barr and Sheriff Bill Eldon. Or, for that matter, there was Hammett's own 1924 *Black Mask* story, "The Man Who Killed Dan Odams." Indeed some of the critics have argued credibly that a direct line of descent connects the mythic figure of the Old West's gun-toting marshal with that popular twentieth-century figure, the private investigator. Both wage a lonely battle as the champions of law and order, matching their wits and their fast draws with the forces of evil that continually threaten to drag a society with a tenuous hold on civilization into chaos, while their less courageous neighbors sleep the sleep of the innocent. He has been invited to Corkscrew, shrugs Hammett's unflappable detective, "to make this part of Arizona ladylike."

And not a moment too soon, it seems. The God-fearing citizens of Corkscrew, led by a Bible-waving, brimstone-spouting reformer named Reverend Dierks, present him with a long list of men they credit with committing some sixty crimes ranging "from murder to intoxication and the use of profane language." The Op has more specific reasons for being in town. He has been hired by a land development company that is having trouble getting farmers to move into the area because of its lawless reputation. The undesirable element seems to be attracted to the lucrative trade of smuggling hopeful immigrants over the border. These seedy entrepreneurs are not above occasionally plundering their clients and leaving them for the buzzards, or even ditching the "evidence" whenever the border police show up. The Op, in short, is up against as ruthless a bunch of hombres as ever Wyatt Earp faced at the O. K. Corral. And like Earp, he must have his Doc Holliday—in this case, a strong, silent cowpoke with the enchanting name of Milk River.

Once again out of his element, Hammett's citified sleuth must endure the taunting of these rough characters like any dude. He wins River's grudging respect not by taming a wild bronco assigned him as a mount but by climbing back on the lethal nag only to be painfully dumped three times in ten minutes. The Op knows the value of symbolic gestures. "Your friends among the better element don't seem to think a whole lot of that trick of yours of giving Big 'Nacio's guns, and his hombres', to Bardell to keep," Milk River chides him. "The general opinion seems to be you took the guns out of their right hands and put 'em back in the left."

"I only took 'em to show that I could," says the detective.

In a place fraught with chronic suspicion and mutual distrust, these two men of few words quickly form a relationship character-ized by an implicit and unspoken affection. They know little of one another. It is a gut thing, though the matter of Milk River's own involvement in local events is uncomfortably hinted at.

The mystery woman is here, too, in the form of another transplanted city-type named Clio Landes. But her sole function in this story seems to be primarily to come between the two men, providing an occasion for them to touch, if only for a fleeting moment, more intimately. When the Op is nearly killed in an authentic High Noon shoot-out with Milk River—she confesses having tampered with his gun to save the man she loves—the cowpoke brutally excoriates her and shows his only moment of emotion, indeed of tenderness, in the story—to his fallen comrade.

> He dropped down beside me, his face a boy's face. A tear fell hot on my hand. "Chief, I didn't—"
> "That's all right," I assured him, and meant it.

This kind of closeness between two men runs through American popular culture from Natty Bumppo and Chingachgook (in James Fenimore Cooper's Leatherstocking novels) to Butch Cassidy and the Sundance Kid. Curiously, one is always a city slicker type, the other a "noble savage" wise in the ways of the wilderness, notes Leslie Fiedler in his famous essay, "Come Back to the Raft Ag'in, Huck Honey," and the distrust of women is usually a subtheme: "the pure love of man and man . . . set off against the ignoble passion of man for woman. . . ."

"Going from the larger cities out into the remote rural communities," Hammett once wrote in a magazine piece given the title "From the Memoirs of a Private Detective," "one finds a steadily decreasing percentage of crimes that have to do with money and a proportionate increase in the frequency of sex as a criminal motive." The Op's excursion into the wild west would seem to disprove that theory. The better element's ostracism of Clio Landes on general principle notwithstanding, Corkscrew's troubles all stem from the greed of the smugglers. Indeed, the latest rash of killings was started, it turns out, over the royal sum of a dollar and ten cents. That, and the mutual distrust of the local factions which over the years had taken on the dimensions of outright paranoia.

Just as "The Scorched Face" looks forward to *The Dain Curse* in its fascination with the morbid cult mentality, "Corkscrew" foreshadows Hammett's other novel of 1929, *Red Harvest*, in which the Op is hired to "cleanse" a lawless town known fittingly as "Poisonville." But before moving on to the larger form, Hammett would flex his wings once more—and the Op's as well—with a short novel (slightly under 40,000 words) that eventually became known by the title of *Blood Money*. Not published in book form until 1943, this early work of Hammett's first appeared in 1927 in the pages of *Black Mask* magazine in two installments—the pair of stories Lillian Hellman chose to conclude the *Knockover* volume. (The novel fragment she has entitled *Tulip*, which comes from a much later period in Hammett's life and is not a detective story at all, will be dealt with briefly in Chapter 10.) Turning on many of the same themes and preoccupations that characterize the other Op stories, they together represent a tour de force of Hammett's by now well-formed twenties style. Though more than half a century has passed since they were written, they provide an unforgettable glimpse of a brutal and slightly crazy era.

They also represent a major escalation of the gangland violence and terrorism that occur in other Hammett stories such as "The Girl With the Silver Eyes" and "The Whosis Kid" into something terrible and almost unrestrained. Half a dozen years into its "great experiment" with prohibition, America was fast breeding a nation-wide cancer of organized crime that grew ever more powerful and brazen in the acting-out of its insatiable ambitions. Small local fiefdoms of illegal enterprise had mushroomed into ever-expanding empires of vice over which underworld czars struggled and intrigued like imperial potentates. Chicago was cut up like a war zone. "On the south side there was Capone and Johnny Torrio. Bugs Moran had the north side," recalls a former PR man for heavyweight champion Jack Dempsey (1919-1926) who was working at the Chicago stadium at the time. "You [had to] allocate the tickets for the boxing shows. Third, fourth, fifth rows center, so many on a side." Capone's men had gunned down rival mobster Dion O'Banion in his flowershop in 1924. Thompson submachine guns were first used by mobs in Chicago's 1925 "beer" wars. The citizenry felt itself increasingly at the mercy of these ruthless gangs. Their combined firepower and criminal expertise loomed as an awesome specter.

In "The Big Knockover" (February 1927) Hammett gave all too vivid form to one of the worst fantasies. Two San Francisco banks are hit simultaneously in broad daylight by more than one hundred fifty gangsters armed with everything from submachine guns to grenades. Sixteen policemen and a dozen bystanders are killed, dozens more injured, leaving a city stunned. But the violence is not over. Fourteen of the gunmen are subsequently found slain in a house on Fillmore Street, and six more in another house. So appalling was the mass violence of Hammett's new story that *Black Mask*'s new editor "Cap" Shaw felt compelled to preface it with an apologia. He cited the recent real-life examples of "gang warfare in Illinois, the big mail-truck holdup in Jersey" which had seen "bandits using airplanes, bombs and machine guns." He admitted Hammett's newest fiction was "stunning in its scope . . . yet can anyone be sure it isn't likely to occur?"

"The Big Knockover" is told in an authoritative voice. It lunges forward with a fierce compulsiveness and a kind of cold nervous energy. Hammett's gift for imagining colorful, wonderfully authentic underworld types seems almost to run wild:

There was the Dis-and-Dat Kid, who had crushed out of Leavenworth only two months before; Sheeny Holmes; Snohomish Shitey, supposed to have died a hero in France in 1919; L.A. Slim, from Denver [sic], sockless and underwearless as usual, with a thousand-dollar bill sewed in each shoulder of his coat; Spider Girrucci wearing a steel-mesh vest under his shirt and a scar from crown to chin where his brother had carved him years ago; Old Pete Best, once a congressman; Nigger Vojan, who once won $175,000 in a Chicago crap game— *Abracadabra* tattooed on him in three places; Alphabet Shorty Mc-Coy; Tom Brooks, Alphabet Shorty's brother-in-law, who invented the Richmond razzle-dazzle and bought three hotels with the profits; . . . Bull McGonickle, still pale from fifteen years in Joliet; Toby the Lugs, Bull's running-mate, who used to brag about picking President Wilson's pocket in a Washington vaudeville theatre; and Paddy the Mex.

Hammett evokes these tough characters well and captures their cocky, often nervous talk.

But the action unreels so fast and furious there is scarcely any time for the kind of brooding or dwelling on character that readers had come to associate with the Op, who punches and shoots his way through this adventure with a frightening zest. He hardly seems the same man who complained in "Corkscrew" that the "proper place for guns is after talk has failed, and I hadn't run out of words by any means when this brown-skinned lad had gone into action." The "Knockover" Op seems indeed to have run out of something. "Don't hesitate," he muses to the reader, finding himself in the midst of a melee, "don't look for targets. God will see to it that there's always a mug there for your gun or blackjack to sock, a belly for your foot." Indeed the several references to religion with which this tale is oddly punctuated are distillations of a cynical theology:

I've got horny skin all over what's left of my soul.

While I pretended to read I wondered whether it would be to my advantage to tell the girl the story was a fake. But I couldn't see any clear profit in that, so I saved my soul a lie.

I weighed them—truth against lie, lie against truth. Once more truth triumphed.

... I went back to my hiding place and hefted the lead pipe, wondering
if Flora had shot me and I was now enjoying the rewards of my
virtue—in a heaven where I could enjoy myself forever and ever
socking folks who had been rough with me down below.

There is even a gangster's moll with the unlikely name of Angel
Grace Cardigan. And in the long description of the Old Man quoted
earlier (and which Hammett liked so much he lifted it intact for his
first novel published two years later), the Op tells us he and his
fellow detectives called their boss "Pontius Pilate among ourselves,
because he smiled politely when he sent us out to be crucified on
suicidal jobs."

This odd preoccupation with a perverted religious imagery in
"The Big Knockover" is echoed, even more oddly, in the closing
scene of the sequel, "$106,000 Blood Money." (The title refers to
the bounty offered for the capture of the man behind the great bank
heist, whom the Op has unwittingly allowed to escape at the end of
the first installment.) The Op has just explained to his boss the
circumstances under which another Continental agent—who it
turned out had been in league with the missing gangster—was killed
in the line of duty. He assures us that he "didn't have anything to
confess" to the Old Man, whose thoughts the Op suddenly finds
himself able to read "for the first time in the years I had known
him." The agency has been spared a grave embarrassment, and the
Old Man, in extending his hand with a grateful "grandfatherly"
smile, seems to be under the impression that the Op arranged the
fortuitous death—a charge of which the younger man seems anxious
to clear his soul, if only for the sake of his private sense of honor.

> "Thank you," he said.
> I took his hand, and I understood him, but I didn't have anything I
> wanted to confess—even by silence.
> "It happened that way," I said deliberately. "I played the cards so
> we would get the benefit of the breaks—but it just happened that way."
> He nodded, smiling benignantly.

The exhaustion the Op describes in the closing lines of the story
may have to do with the sheer enormity of the operation around
which this adventure turned—it may even reflect, on some level,
Hammett's own fatigue from having written his first 40,000-word

story—but probably also with the ever-increasing toll all this hard-boiled swashbuckling is taking on the middle-aged detective. In "The Big Knockover" he reminds us again of his age (forty) and makes no fewer than *five* direct references to the fact that he is overweight and less inclined to exert himself than he once was. (Is the Op, as novelist John Updike once said of himself, exhausted by the memory of his former energy?) Is he getting too old for the cruel game he has been trained to play so well? Is he feeling discouraged at the growing realization that he will never really be completely at home with it, even after all he has been through?

"Nellie," says Paddy the Mex at the very beginning of the story, evidently with some genuine affection, "meet the biggest-hearted dick in San Francisco. This little fat guy will do anything for anybody," he adds by way of a little gallows humor, "if only he can send 'em over for life in the end." The Op joins in the laughter. He has recognized "Nellie" as Angel Grace Cardigan, a young bunco artist he had run to the ground six years before in Philadelphia. Angel—who was nineteen at the time and escaped conviction because none of her male victims would bring charges against her—remembers the Op, she tells him later, as "one white [meaning *understanding* and *decent*] dick!"

Paddy's offhand remark takes on significance in the light of what happens in this story. The brains behind the operation doesn't just escape. He is allowed by the Op to sneak out past the arriving police because the detective has been taken in by the archvillain's pitiful portrayal. When the dying Bluepoint Vance reveals the truth, the Op is stunned.

> His words ran out. He shuddered. Death wasn't a sixteenth of an inch behind his eyes. A white-coated intern tried to get past me into the car. I pushed him out of the way and leaned in taking Vance by the shoulders. The back of my neck was ice. My stomach was empty.

The fact that "$106,000 Blood Money" begins with Paddy the Mex's brother coming to the Op with a fresh lead—nay, being sent to him by Angel Grace Cardigan because "you were . . . a good guy for a sleuth"—is clearly intended as a piece of irony. If he had not been such a mensch in the first place, no sequel would have been necessary. The Op pursues the rest of the gang now with renewed cynicism and impatience at any suggestion of human weakness.

"Stop spoofing!" he scowls at his fellow agent's explanation of how he got involved with a millionairess named Ann Newall and her crooked friend, a Greek named Papadopoulos. ("He showed me how we together could accumulate unheard-of piles of wealth. So there you are," the young man says, speaking to one of the Op's favorite themes, "The prospect of all that money completely devastated my morals."

> Stop spoofing! The money Papadopoulos showed you didn't buy you. You met the girl and were too soft to turn her in. But your vanity— your pride in looking at yourself as a pretty cold proposition— wouldn't let you admit it even to yourself. You had to have a hard-boiled front. . . . [Papadopoulos] gave you a part you could play to yourself.

The Op might be talking to himself, though he shows no signs of realizing it. "That's the way you went, my son," he continues, mimicking the diction of a father confessor. "You went as far as possible beyond what was needed to save the girl from the hoosegow—just to show the world, but chiefly yourself, that you were not acting through sentimentality, but according to your own reckless desires. There you are, " he finishes, "Look at yourself."

The Op is so sharp with the younger man because he has felt the same tendencies in himself, and they scared him to death. He realizes that he too has fled behind the armor—and the self-deception—of a "hard-boiled" front when his feelings were about to get the better of him. The Dark Lady of so many of the Op stories symbolizes in a way another side of himself he is afraid to know or to acknowledge—but to which he is forever and relentlessly drawn. To be able to trust this character completely would be to realize the fullness of his humanity, finally to be whole; but having seen too much of the evil of the world, he does not dare let down his guard. So he has learned instead to act a role that will keep him safe, though it is to accept a kind of death.

And in "$106,000 Blood Money" the Op in his turn has given his fellow agent "a part to play," literally, to the point of getting him to dress up in a tux for the story's final, violent confrontation scene—that ends with the agent's death. ("Yeah," I said sourly, "I'm another Papadopoulos.")

Filing his report back at the office, the Op says that he suddenly "understood" the Old Man for the first time. "We who worked under him were proud of his cold-bloodedness," he had said earlier. In his efforts to redeem himself from a set of circumstances set in motion by an act of mercy—letting Papadopoulos escape the first time—Hammett's detective has committed the most cold-blooded act of his life. "I played the cards so we would get the benefit of the breaks," he tells the Old Man, characterizing himself as the deliberate, emotionless poker player. Nothing "a couple of weeks off" won't fix. But his closing sentence to the reader is stripped of even the smallest pretense of the old, habitual bravado. "I felt tired," he confides, "washed out." It is just possible that what he is most exhausted from of all is the struggle of continually trying to reconcile the contradictions in his own character.

6
The Evil That Men Do:
Red Harvest

> Midway upon the journey of our life
> I found that I was in a dusky wood;
> For the right path, whence I had strayed, was lost.
> Ah me! How hard a thing it is to tell
> The wildness of that rough and savage place. . . .
>
> —*Canto I, Dante's Inferno*

Another familiar pattern appears in *Blood Money*, that of the rich kid who falls in with a bad crowd; or more specifically, in this case, the well-educated daughter of a wealthy family who becomes romantically involved with a tough-talking primitive-type gangster. In "Fly Paper" Sue Hambleton ran with one Babe McCloor, a brawny gunman who "was resting up after doing a fifteen-year hitch in Leavenworth for ruining most of the smaller post offices between New Orleans and Omaha" and "was keeping himself in drinking money by playing with pedestrians in dark streets." In *Blood Money* a millionaire's daughter is infatuated with the mobster Red O'Leary. "He was so gloriously a roughneck," Hammett tells us, "that she saw him as a romantic figure."

> They met often. He took her to all the rowdy holes in the bay district, introduced her to yeggs, gunmen, swindlers, told her wild tales of

criminal adventuring. She knew he was a crook, knew he was tied up in the Seamen's National and Golden Gate Trust jobs when they broke. But she saw it all as a sort of theatrical spectacle. She didn't see it as it was.

This last sentence is the important one. Hammett was making the same point that would be made a generation later in the 1968 film classic *Bonnie and Clyde* and again, still more powerfully, in *The Godfather*. It is too easy to forget that these romantic, occasionally even dashing types make their living by killing and maiming people; that their swashbuckling adventures regularly involve the pain and suffering of other human beings; and that the reality is not very pretty to look at. The grisly episode reported by the Op in *Blood Money*—of the naked man who had stumbled into the Market Street shopping district with strips of flesh hanging from his torso—is meant to be shocking. But it is not a gratuitous depiction of violence included merely for effect. It was precisely this hideous act on the part of her gangster friends, we learn later, that "sickened" Angel Grace—who was neither rich girl nor angel—to the point where she decided to send Paddy the Mex's brother to the Op. It was responsible, in other words, for reopening the case.

If readers of crime fiction had become inured to the "infinite cruelty" of murder, Hammett would have to find some other way to bring the point home, to make us, along with Angel Grace Cardigan and her friend Ann Newall, experience the world of the Red O'Learys "as it was."

Even if one may sometimes doubt, as Raymond Chandler did, "that Hammett had any deliberate artistic aims whatever," his concern with getting the realities of the world of cops and robbers he had known on paper is unquestionable; Hammett's letters to the editor and book reviews, written in his own voice, underscore this desire.

The brutal actions of that world no longer surprise the Op. A 3:00 A.M. phone call from another detective barely interrupts his sleep. "Exit Arlie," says the voice on the other end matter-of-factly, reporting the most recent killing.

"R.I.P.?"
"Yep."

"How?"
"Lead."
"Our lad's?"
"Yep."
"Keep till morning?"
"Yep."
"See you at the office," and I went back to sleep.

What *does* surprise the Op are those moments in which he suddenly discovers a softer side in the hard-bitten criminals he pursues, some disturbing remnant of their humanity.

[Flora's] big body suddenly quivered. Pain clouded her handsome brutal face. Two tears came out of her lower eyelids.
I'm damned if she hadn't loved the old scoundrel!

In the end, it is the complexity of evil that unnerves him. And its insidiousness. The fact that it can turn up, like DDT, in the blood-stream of the good guys and slowly, little by little, take over their lives, even as they rationalize their actions to the world and to themselves with the noblest of interpretations. In *Blood Money* it is a promising young fellow agent the Op sees this happen to; in *Red Harvest*, it is himself.

The very name of the town in which this first of Hammett's full-length novels is set becomes a metaphor for this insidious process: Personville, a fictional town of 40,000 supposedly located near Ogden, Utah, is known as "Poisonville," we are told in the book's first sentence, by the tough-talking hoodlum types who control it—a piece of gallows humor, the Op says, that was to prove strangely fitting in the light of his own adventures there.

He has been brought here, as he was to the frontier town of Corkscrew, to clean up a criminal element which has the good citizenry in thrall. Indeed *Red Harvest* is in many ways an arche-typal western in modern-urban dress. But there is little of the comedy that characterized the earlier story. The tone of this assign-ment is altogether more serious. There is a further important differ-ence. In "Corkscrew" the Op had been hired by a coldly commer-cial concern interested only in redeeming the commercial value of its property; the self-righteous citizens' group that tries to assume the role of his employer is made the butt of much humor. In *Red*

Harvest the Op has been sent for by a crusading young newspaper publisher named Donald Willsson, who is killed shortly after the detective arrives.

The effect of this sudden development is twofold: it leaves the Op in the position of having to step into the ill-fitting shoes of Personville's prematurely slain redeemer, and it puts him in the predicament (a favorite of Hammett's) of now having to piece together the situation from what other people tell him.

Arriving on the scene of the murder he picks out a rumpled, "intelligent" looking man in a red tie to explain to him what has happened. "Don Willsson's gone to sit on the right hand of God," the detective is told in one of Hammett's lovely brutal-lyrical one-liners of hard-boiled compassion, "if God don't mind looking at bullet holes."

Recognizing the man's scarlet cravat as the emblem of the Industrial Workers of the World, a leftist labor union, the nameless Op rummages through his wallet for an appropriate identity among a selection of bogus business cards he carries and comes up with a red IWW card. "It identified me as Henry F. Neil, AB seaman, member in good standing of the Industrial Workers of the World. There wasn't a word of truth in it," the Op quickly adds, lest his readers jump to the conclusion that their hero had finally revealed his true identity. (Actually, his handy "collection of credentials" had been a regular tool of Hammett's trade back in his Pinkerton days.) He seems almost relieved when the man, whose name is Bill Quint, is not taken in by the card, though he pretends to be; the Op trustingly confides, with hard-boiled humor, that he has other cards in his wallet. The two men are soon talking over (illegal) whiskey together, sharing a sweetly distanced but genuine rapport reminiscent of the Op's friendship with Milk River. Hammett clearly respects this character.

The detective has picked Quint out of the crowd for a reason. The red tie "interested" him. The first thing the Op had noticed on arriving in Personville had been "the smelters whose brick stacks stuck up tall against a gloomy mountain to the south [which] had yellow-smoked everything into a uniform dinginess." Personville is a mining town—"an ugly city of forty thousand people, set in an ugly notch between two ugly mountains that had been all dirtied up by mining." Mines meant unions. And together they meant trouble.

The International Workers of the World, or "wobblies," were associated in the 1920's with bitter violence and struggles, the result of newly organized workers trying to wrest new standards of fairness from powerful employers long accustomed to having their own way. Impassioned rhetoric, mass walkouts, bomb throwing, strikes, labor meetings broken up by company-paid goons, rumors of radical conspiracies to subvert capitalism multiplied alarmingly in the years following World War One. "There was an unmistakable trend," wrote Frederick Lewis Allen, "toward socialistic ideas both in the ranks of labor and among liberal intellectuals. The Socialist Party, watching the success of the Russian Revolution, was flirting with the idea of violent mass-action." The rights of workers were preached aggressively in inner city slum and factory town, until the average citizen, says Allen, was no longer sure who were the bad guys and who were the good guys. Remarking that "these profiteers are about as bad as the IWW's" was as strong a statement as one could make.

The fear of bolsheviks soon resulted in tightening immigration policies to limit the influx of undesirable aliens, as well as the combing of textbooks for slights to heroes of American history and the unabashed censoring of public speakers. By 1922 an article in *Harper's Magazine* could lament that "America is no longer a free country, in the old sense." The red scare had reached such proportions by the summer of 1927 that a shoemaker named Nicola Sacco and a fish peddler named Bartolomeo Vanzetti, who had been active in Boston anarchist circles, could be sentenced to death by electrocution by a right-wing judge who boasted openly, amid fierce public debate and protest, that he was going to make an example of them.

Bill Quint's red tie surely called up all these associations in the readers who sat down to the first installment of Hammett's novel that November in the pages of *Black Mask*. The very title Hammett chose for the book version published two years later no doubt played deliberately, in its tantalizing ambiguity, with his readers' expectations of leftist worker violence.

The "poison" in the entrails of Personville, the Op learns from Quint, does indeed go back to the bitter coal miner strikes of 1921.

For forty years old Elihu Willsson—father of the man who had been killed this night—had owned Personville, heart, soul, skin and guts. He was president and majority stockholder of the Personville Mining Corporation, ditto of the First National Bank, owner of the *Morning Herald* and *Evening Herald*, the city's only newspapers. . . . Along with these pieces of property he owned a United States senator, a couple of representatives, the governor, the mayor, and most of the state legislature. Elihu Willsson was Personville, and he was almost the whole state.

This last is an important point. To Hammett the "poison" is present, at least in embryo, in old Willsson. During the prosperous war years, he had given in to his newly organized workers' demands. When coal prices dropped in 1921, the old capitalist— referred to as the *Czar* of Poisonville—had arrogantly torn up his agreements with the miners, and a bloody eight-month-long strike had ensued. Old Elihu had crushed the revolt, but he had lost his hold on the city and the state in the process. The thugs he had hired to put down the miners had gotten a taste of power and they liked it; they had taken the city for their spoils. Up to his own ears in corruption, and unable to withstand too much scrutiny, old Willsson could not afford to break openly with them.

The ironies were redoubled. The old industrialist's idealistic son, innocent of his father's involvement, had come home from Europe to take command of the city's two newspapers and embarked on a campaign of civic reform. Though the elder Willsson ostensibly blames his son's death on young Donald's wife, it soon begins to appear as though the local racketeers were behind it.

The old man hires the Op to find the killer or killers and to clean up Personville. "I'd have to have a free hand—no favors to anybody—run the job as I pleased," says the detective, reading the old man's motives; he is being used to break the back of Willsson's enemies just as, to Quint's way of thinking, young Donald was being used. When the chips are down his client can be trusted no more than any other crook in the vicinity. Once again the Op is surrounded by villains. Before long he will be ducking into doorways, dodging a rain of bullets, unable to count even on the police, who have long since been bought.

Enter the dark lady.

"Who is this Dinah Brand?" asks the Op of the jovial chief of police. "A soiled dove," replies the puckish Irishman. "a de luxe hustler, a big-league gold-digger." A mysterious check for $5,000 hand-delivered to her house by Donald Willsson on the night of his murder leads the Op to her door. Chief Noonan's revelation that she is the girl friend of Max "Whisper" Thaler, a local gambling casino owner and prime suspect in the murder, marks her as dangerous. But in the space of a few pages, Hammett has reduced—or complicated—our sense of who this woman is to a tangle of ambiguities.

An interview with Willsson's widow corroborates Noonan's characterization of Dinah Brand as some sort of villainess. Then a young bank teller and former admirer admits she is "money-mad, all right, but somehow you don't mind it. She's so thoroughly mercenary, so frankly greedy, that there's nothing disagreeable about it." Hammett has already begun to paint her in the kind of terms he finds likable—excesses are somehow less offensive to him if one is frank about them, owns them for what they are. Though they had an enjoyable relationship, he says, she stopped seeing him when he began flirting with embezzlement to feed her expensive tastes. "I wanted you to know she has her good side too," says the young man. "You'll hear enough about the other." ("Or maybe," suggests the ever-skeptical Op, "it was just that she didn't think she'd get enough to pay for the risk of being caught in a jam.") But then there is Dan Rolff, a sickly "lunger" (tuberculosis sufferer) Dinah lets live in her house, evidently out of compassion, and now supports—an even stronger hint on Hammett's part that this mysterious lady is something less than a villainess, while Bill Quint, now revealed as a former suitor who allegedly "threatened to kill her," is suddenly suspect.

When the reader finally sees her, it is through the Op's eyes. She is a couple of inches taller than he is ("which made her about five feet eight"). At twenty-five, "Little lines crossed the corners of her big ripe mouth. Fainter lines were beginning to make nets around her thick-lashed eyes. They were large eyes, blue and a bit bloodshot." She is not, in short, what one would expect in a heroine.

> Her coarse hair—brown—needed trimming and was parted crookedly. One side of her upper lip had been rouged higher than the other. Her

dress was of a particularly unbecoming wine color, and it gaped here and there down one side, where she had neglected to snap the fasteners or they had popped open. There was a run down the front of her left stocking.

The Op almost seems to relish the incongruity of it all. "This was the Dinah Brand," he reflects, "who took her pick of Poisonville's men, according to what I'd been told."

Yet the hand she holds out to him is "soft, warm, strong"— characteristics we have seen Hammett admires. By the time, four pages later, the reader finally hears *her* version of things, he is torn between the damning fact of her association with Whisper and her innate likableness. "You'll be disappointed at first. Then, without being able to say how or when it happened," the young teller had predicted, "you'll find you've forgotten your disappointment, and the first thing you know you'll be telling her your life's history, and all your troubles and hopes."

It is not long before the Op is doing exactly that. He will become deeply troubled in the course of this adventure about his own motives and methods. With his shrewd gamester's skill, he pits gangsters against cops, gangsters against gangsters, passing little explosive bits of information—or misinformation—along to one or the other as his purpose suits him "just to see what would happen," then slipping out the back way while the town's inflamed elements go at one another. When Dinah remarks on his "vague way of doing things," he explains his modus operandi. "Plans are all right some-times," he tells her. "And sometimes just stirring things up is all right—if you're tough enough to survive, and keep your eyes open so you'll see what you want when it comes to the top."

When men start to die, the Op discovers to his growing horror that he actually enjoys his role, describing himself with merry malice as "juggling death and destruction." He confides these disturbing realizations to Dinah Brand. "I've arranged a killing or two in my time, when they were necessary. But this is the first time I ever got the fever. . . . Play with murder long enough and it gets you one of two ways. It makes you sick, or you get to like it."

He blames it on the city itself. ("It's this damned town. Poison-ville is right. It's poisoned me.") But he knows better. And when she agrees with him—"It's not your fault, darling. You said yourself that there was nothing else you could do"—he snaps back: "There was plenty else I could do. . . . But it's easier to have them killed off, easier and surer, and . . . more satisfying." He is horrified at the spectacle of his own indifference to the human suffering he himself has brought about, and says:

> Look. I sat at Willsson's table tonight and played them like you'd play trout, and got just as much fun out of it. I looked at Noonan and knew he hadn't a chance in a thousand of living another day because of what I had done to him, and I laughed, and felt warm and happy inside. That's not me. I've got hard skin all over what's left of my soul, and after twenty years of messing around with crime I can look at any sort of a murder without seeing anything in it but my bread and butter, the day's work.

Again and again she offers him ways out of his moral dilemma. "You exaggerate so, honey. They deserve all they get." But his own phrases seem to haunt him. *What's left of my soul. The day's work. That's not me.* This is a long way from the Op's self-righteous ranting about his pleasure in his work in "The Gutting of Couffignal." In the hardcover version of *Red Harvest* Hammett underscores his hero's moral agony with the touching words about his "soul" from "The Big Knockover" and borrows a striking description of the Old Man, slightly rewritten, from the same story:

> The Old Man was the manager of the Continental's San Francisco branch. He was also known as Pontius Pilate, because he smiled pleasantly when he sent us out to be crucified on suicidal jobs. He was a gentle, polite, elderly person with no more warmth than a hangman's rope. The Agency wits said he could spit icicles in July.

Once again the specter of the Old Man's total cynicism, his loveless soul, looms before the Op as a haunting reminder of what he fears he will become. (The fact that Hammett returns again and again to this imagery snows its thematic importance to him.) "It's right enough for the Agency to have rules and regulations," the Op is telling fellow operative Mickey Linehan on the next page, "but when you're out on a job you've got to do it the best way you can. And anybody that brings any ethics to Poisonville is going to get them all rusty." Five chapters later the Op's flinty pragmatism has given way to racking self-doubts and anxious soliloquies to Dinah Brand, the

only person in Personville with whom he can talk openly. Even
Linehan and Dick Foley, his fellow ops—especially his fellow ops—
are told nothing of all this.

At forty—"fat, middle-aged, hard-boiled"—the Op, like Dante,
midway upon his life's journey, has wandered from the path of
certainty and begun his season in hell. Dinah worries aloud that he is
headed for a "nervous breakdown." Hammett's hero is drinking
more than usual in this novel, it soon becomes apparent, and he is
drinking to get drunk. He senses that he too is becoming a murderer
inside, moving closer and closer to what he is fighting, until he will
be indistinguishable from his enemy.

On the last night when he and Dinah sit down together before
she is killed the two are drinking gin doped with laudanum. The first
dream the Op dreams that night is about chasing a woman who is
somehow "important to me." His second dream is a terrible one: He
is struggling high above the upturned faces of a crowd with a dark
little man; too late he realizes he has gone off the edge of the roof
with him and is falling toward the crowd.

It is not that he will die in Personville that the Op fears, it is that
he has lost himself, the person that he was, in the process of
destroying his enemies.

Waking from his drug-induced dream he discovers—an even
greater shock—that he has lost the one person he trusted. His
fingers are curled around an ice pick stuck into the breast of Dinah
Brand. The rest of the book is a waking nightmare in which he hunts
for her murderer, not entirely sure, he will later admit, that it is not
himself. Calmly, with cold efficiency, he obliterates his fingerprints,
removes all evidence pointing to his own guilt. If he feels any grief at
the death of this close friend, that too is suppressed.

But, with all that has happened, with all that he has felt, the Op
does not go to pieces; instead he refuses to accept the obvious—
that he himself, in the depths of his degradation, was responsible for
Dinah's death. Instead he clings to the commonsense methods he
has learned as a detective—for which he needs moral distance, not
self-pity and the distortions of guilt. One by one he explores the
possible scenarios. The key again is experience. His familiarity with
"hopheads" and their drug-induced hallucinations has led him to
suspect that his "dreams" that night might have been something

more than mere dreams, rather some kind of distorted perception of things going on in the same room. The fact that the lights had been turned out—a fact that the detective, with his long-ingrained habit of careful observation, had noticed upon waking—had strongly suggested a third party at least had come and gone.

The facts that eventually come to light are typical of Hammett's realism. The killer had not come there with the intention of murdering Dinah, but on another mission entirely; she had been slain almost by accident. That Hammett, in contrast to most of the so-called classic mystery writers, passes over any number of people who had very acceptable motives for murdering Dinah Brand, reflects his concern with writing detective stories that were faithful to the way things happen, as often as not, in the real world. When similarly it turns out that Donald Willsson was slain neither by organized crime nor ideology-crazed anarchists, but by a distraught young man over a woman, Hammett is deliberately flying in the face of his readers' expectations. The novel is, as John G. Cawelti points out in his fine essay on the book, no mere "political parable—Personville being a symbol of the exploitative capitalist society that has reached the point where its internal contradictions keep it in a state of perpetual corruption and chaos. Such a reading might fit the details of the novel and our knowledge of Hammett's personal ideological commitments, but it seems basically irrelevant to *Red Harvest.*" Instead Cawelti sees Hammett, underneath his radicalism, as "a bleak and stoical pessimist with no more real faith in a revolutionary utopia to come than in existing societies."

The fact is that by its closing pages the novel has vividly made its point about "exploitative capitalist society." Does Hammett really expect us to believe the Op's assertion that the Personville he leaves behind is "developing into a sweetsmelling thornless bed of roses"? (He is paraphrasing Mickey Linehan's words.) Or is this not just one more instance of the Op's hard-boiled sense of humor? ("I haven't laughed so much over anything," he tells Elihu Willsson a few pages earlier, "since the hogs ate my kid brother.") But *Red Harvest* is more concerned finally with making a far subtler point—a perception that both underlies and goes beyond Hammett's pessimism where society is concerned.

Old Willsson merely wants to regain control of these evil forces for his own ends; he refuses to see them for what they are and to acknowledge his own *complicity* with them. The Op by contrast has been struggling painfully with precisely these questions where his own espousal of evil in the name of destroying evil was concerned. And if in the end he himself chooses to cover up his own complicity with the evil in this world, he knows that someone else sees through his manipulation of the facts.

> I spent most of my week in Ogden trying to fix up my reports so they would not read as if I had broken as many Agency rules, state laws and human bones as I had. . . . I might just as well have saved the labor and sweat. . . . They didn't fool the Old Man. He gave me merry hell.

And if the punishment doled out by the cynical god of the Op's universe is a somewhat "merrier" hell than the one Hammett's childhood religion described, that too is beside the point. The Op has already known the flames of that dreadful city of the heart Dante wrote of.

> *Thus we descended the dark scarp of Hell*
> *to which all the evil of the Universe*
> *comes home at last, into the Fourth Great Circle*

> *And ledge of the abyss. O Holy Justice,*
> *who could relate the agonies I saw!*
> *What guilt is man that he can come to this?*
>
> —Canto IV, *The Inferno*, Ciardi trans.

"As Dante used his native Florence as a model for hell," observes William Nolan, "so Hammett utilized Poisonville." Nolan's highly suggestive analogy is worth pursuing: Personville is a place brimming not only with crime and political corruption but with all manner of human passions and jealousies, concupiscence as well as cupidity, hypocrisy and inhumanity, tarnished saints (Bill Quint) and sentimental sinners (Dinah Brand). Dinah, who plays a tattered Beatrice to the Op's Dante, takes the destitute and pitiable Dan Rolff in out of the kindness of her heart, but she also slaps him around and humiliates him in front of other men when her own selfish needs get the better of her. The dark satanic mills that greeted the Op on his arrival in Personville pale before these far somberer realities.

The flip bravado of the novel's ending notwithstanding, Hammett's hero has been deeply shaken. He has glimpsed a frightful truth: that in the end evil springs not merely from greed or organized crime or even passionate ideologies but from the pragmatism of people. It springs from the eternal willingness of human beings to compromise their ideals and betray their nobler impulses to satisfy their baser needs—from having one's own way (old Elihu), to escaping discovery (Dinah's murderer), to . . . revenge. "Your fat chief of police tried to assassinate me last night," the Op tells Elihu Willsson at what is to be the turning point of this adventure. "I'm just mean enough to want to ruin him for it. Now I'm going to have my fun. I've got ten thousand dollars of your money to play with. I'm going to use it opening Poisonville up from Adam's apple to ankles." What began as a job has now taken on the character of "me versus Poisonville."

But before he is done the Op is recoiling in horror from his own glee in plotting its destruction. *That's not me,* he tells Dinah Brand. This "getting a rear [kick] out of planning deaths is not natural to me. It's what *this place* has done to me" (italics mine). "This place" is not Personville, but the world. Personville, like Dante's Florence, is only a symbol for human society. It is civilization itself that has corrupted the Op. Hammett's realization is the same as Dante's: Human beings make their own hell.

7
Dead Souls:
The Dain Curse

"It does, as you put it, look like the work of one mind."
The novelist Owen Fitzstephan in The Dain Curse

As Personville's stand-in savior the Op turns in a less-than Christ-like performance. The survivor instincts in him run too deep to accommodate martyrdom.

None of Hammett's heroes dies. But then that is in the nature of the genre to which he chose to restrict himself, or within which he was most comfortable. Whichever way you look at it, the fact is that—in marked contrast to other writers of the hard-boiled school such as Ernest Hemingway, James M. Cain, Horace McCoy, and Nathanael West—Hammett had deliberately limited himself to a type of fiction in which the main character is by definition the survivor, the one who, even if everybody else falls victim to the powers of evil, comes out on top.

Indeed, the ultimate survival of the hero is no doubt one of the satisfactions habitual readers of detective stories seek in the genre. It is something one can count on, come hell or high water. When Conan Doyle tried to kill off Sherlock Holmes the public was outraged—and not only, I suggest, because they wanted more adventures. Doyle had sinned against their deepest sense of order.

87

With Hammett's Op survival has become almost a theme. In *Red Harvest* he explains to Dinah Brand that it is a matter of being "tough enough to survive." And that involves not only stamina but one's very lifestyle. In *Red Harvest*, as in the earlier stories, the Op's style of talking and acting both symbolizes and abets his determination to outlast his foes.

In one memorable scene early on in the book, he has just entered a room. Suddenly he is being shot at from a dark rooftop across the street. "I looked around for something to chuck at the light globe, found a Gideon Bible and chucked it. The bulb popped apart, giving me darkness." If the Op, like his creator, is a tortured idealist who misses the presence of some kind of eternal moral principles in the world, he is also a wily pragmatist who knows that in a world of hypocrisy and evil it is sometimes not in light but in the absence of light that lies one's only chance for survival.

Darkness, oddly enough, was to become the dominant motif of Hammett's next book. The very titles of the original installments in which *The Dain Curse* first appeared between November 1928 and February 1929 in *Black Mask* reflect this preoccupation: "Black Lives," "The Hollow Temple," "Black Honeymoon" and "Black Riddle."

The Op is investigating the disappearance of some diamonds on behalf of an insurance company. As usual, he probes beyond the "obvious" solution, uncovering disconnected threads of some more mysterious goings-on. A key suspect is murdered. Then Edgar Leggett himself, the man from whom the gems were stolen, suddenly turns up dead, accompanied by a strange "suicide" note that opens the door on a sordid family history.

He is in reality, we learn, one Maurice de Mayenne, a fugitive from justice and escapee from Devil's Island who had murdered his first wife and married her sister. Within a handful of pages the Op's keen observation and habitual skepticism have exploded the dead man's story, drawing from Leggett's distraught widow Alice a second, then a third version—each more sinister than the preceding. Some twenty years before in Paris, Mayenne had married a young Englishwoman named Lily Dain, who was pregnant with his child, but secretly loving her sister Alice instead. For almost five years Alice had lusted for her sister's death—until a bizarre accident with a loaded gun in the hand of a five-year-old child ironically brought it about. In Alice Dain's final confession the story grows even more macabre. Alice, it seems, had cold-bloodedly taught the child a morbid "little game" with an unloaded pistol kept in a drawer in her parents' room.

> I would lie on Lily's bed, pretending to sleep. The child would push a chair to the chiffonier, climb up on it, take the pistol from the drawer, creep over to the bed, put the muzzle of the pistol to my head, and press the trigger. When she did it well, making little or no noise, holding the pistol correctly in her tiny hands, I would reward her with candy, cautioning her against saying anything about the game to her mother or to anyone else, as we were going to surprise her mother with it.

On that fateful day, returning home unexpectedly, Mayenne had reached the bedroom door just as little Gabrielle pulled the trigger. The traumatic memory of this monstrous incident was eventually suppressed from the consciousness of the child, who even then, says Alice, showed signs of being mentally deficient. Whether or not drugs were used at the time, the twenty-year-old girl who now stands whimpering under the venomous shower of curses by her hateful stepmother has become a dull-eyed drug addict without a shred of self-respect. She is cursed, Alice Dain Leggett tells her sister's daughter,

> with the same black soul and rotten blood that she [Lily] and I and all the Dains have had; and you're cursed with your mother's blood on your hands in babyhood; and with the twisted mind and the need for drugs that are my gift to you; and your life will be black as your mother's and mine were black; and the lives of those you touch will be black as Maurice's was black.

Within moments Alice Dain is dead, killed in a scuffle during an attempt to make her escape. And so might have ended a tale of horror, murder and frightful revelations of the sort the readers of the pulps had encountered before. But Hammett has only begun.

There is something about the three versions of the Dain family history—indeed about all that has happened—that has left the Op uneasy. "You're never satisfied until you've got two buts and an if attached to everything," an exasperated old acquaintance named

Owen Fitzstephan chides him in the course of the next chapter, aptly entitled "Buts and Ifs," in which the detective worries over the "established facts" as a child would pick at a scab.

Fitzstephan, a novelist the Op had known back east ("We used to drink out of the same bottle"), serves as the Op's confidant throughout *The Dain Curse* in a series of comradely chats which usually take place over beer and supper in his landlady's basement. Together they sift through the facts and analyze the characters, often echoing each other's very phrases. Even when they are arguing, their mutual put-downs seem good-natured. The underlying similarity between a novelist's work and a detective's clearly fascinates them. "Are you—who make your living snooping—sneering at my curiosity about people and my attempts to satisfy it?" asks Fitzstephan.

> "We're different," I said. "I do mine with the object of putting people in jail, and I get paid for it, though not as much as I should."
> "That's not different," he said. "I do mine with the object of putting people in books, and I get paid for it, though not as much as I should."
> "Yeah, but what good does that do?"
> "God knows. What good does putting them in jail do?"

People who knew Hammett must have doubly enjoyed these exchanges since, as William F. Nolan has pointed out, the description we are given of Fitzstephan closely parallels—employing some of the very words and phrases—Hammett's description of himself in a letter of the period. Fitzstephan, we are told, is "a long, lean, sorrel-haired man of thirty-two with sleepy gray eyes, a wide mouth and carelessly worn clothes; a man who pretended to be lazier than he was, would rather talk than do anything else and had a lot of what seemed to be accurate information and original ideas on any subject that happened to come up, as long as it was a little out of the ordinary."

But if Hammett the novelist allows himself to come in for a little kidding, he also takes the opportunity of this "appearance" in one of his own books to poke fun at his paunchy detective and his nose-to-the-grindstone method of forever marshaling "all the facts you can get and turn[ing] them over and over till they click."

"If that's your technic, you'll have to put up with it," Fitzstephan tells the Op. "But I'm damned if I see why I should suffer. You recited the Mayenne-Leggett-Collinson history step by step last night at least half a dozen times. You've done nothing else since breakfast this morning. I'm getting enough of it. Nobody's mysteries ought to be as tiresome as you're making this one."

"Hell," the Op comes back. "I sat up half the night after you went to bed and recited it to myself. You got to turn them over and over, my boy, until they click."

"I like the Nick Carter school better," sniffs Fitzstephan.

The novelist frowns at the detective's determination to find a more prosaic explanation for the Dain family's tragedy than some mysterious "strain in the blood." The detective dismisses the novelist's interpretation of what happened as too "literary." "I'm a novelist," says Fitzstephan. "My business is with souls and what goes on in them." In fact, it is the coexistence of a hard-headed realism with an interest in "souls and what goes on in them" in Hammett himself that makes him an interesting writer and his detective stories more truly novels than most examples of the genre. For the Op's relentless and painstaking methods—along with his poker player's knack for flushing out his opponent's hand—will uncover in the course of this, his second novel, a story of human weaknesses, jealousies, hates, lust, egotism and revenge that reveals Hammett to be a considerable student of human nature.

Like *Red Harvest*, *The Dain Curse* was to be a study in evil. But if the early novelette *Blood Money* and the book that followed it chronicle the Op's own sickening descent into the slough of cynicism, bringing him finally face to face with the fact of his own participation in the world's evil, *The Dain Curse* was to take an even more disturbing look (*pace* André Gide) at atrocity and cynicism. And Hammett placed at its center the most truly satanic of all his villains, the blackest and most completely cynical soul he could imagine: the novelist Owen Fitzstephan.

Indeed the sinister circumstances in which the detective continually finds himself are like bad dreams from which he cannot quite awaken—for the Op has, quite literally, become a character in a plot of Fitzstephan's making. It is the universe of some perverse, morbid god whose dark logic forever eludes one's grasp even as it teases the mind with the shadow of some obscure purpose. "It does, as you put it, look like the work of one mind," Fitzstephan finally agrees with the frustrated detective. "And a goofy one," adds the Op.

But the clues have been there from the beginning, if only we—and the Op—had been able to make the connections. The novel reread after the revelations of the last pages becomes an almost equally sinister story on a wholly different level. In the very second paragraph where the Op introduces his old friend to the reader (in a chapter ominously entitled "Something Black"), the detective reveals he had met him "five years before, in New York, where I was digging dirt on a chain of fake mediums who had taken a coal-and-ice dealer's widow for a hundred thousand dollars. Fitzstephan," says the Op innocently, "was plowing the same field for literary material. We became acquainted and pooled forces. I got more out of the combination than he did, since he knew the spook racket inside and out; and, with his help, I cleaned up my job in a couple of weeks."

Fewer than twenty pages later the Op is ringing the doorbell of a mysterious urban retreat known as the Temple of the Holy Grail. And another thirty pages after that, barely two into the second part of the book ("The Temple"), he is preparing to spend the night in the place—a night he will long if not fondly remember.

Gabrielle Leggett, with her doctor's approval, has taken refuge there with a strange couple known as the Haldorns, friends of her late parents, who have gathered a following of well-heeled society types who seem to find some solace in the druidic rites over which the Elijah-like Joseph Haldorn presides at a thirty-foot-high altar in an atrium open to the stars. The Op has been engaged by Gabrielle's guardian, an attorney named Madison Andrews, to see if his ward is all right. Andrews's skepticism concerning such mystery cults—which enjoyed a great surge of popularity on the coast during the nineteen twenties—is exceeded only by that of the Op himself. "I didn't believe in the supernatural," he says flatly. But even he, to his surprise, finds the Haldorns strangely irresistible.

"[He] looked at you and spoke to you," he tells Fitzstephan of his encounter with the white-haired prophet, "and things happened inside you. I'm not the easiest guy in the world to dazzle, I hope; but he had me going. I came damned near to believing he was God toward the last." But before that first night in the renovated six-story apartment house-cum-temple is over, the Op will experience things that seem to fall beyond the normal definition of the real: an incorporeal apparition with which he struggles desperately for his life in a tiny room, a man whom bullets pass through but cannot stop, bloody daggers and disappearing bodies, but most of all the truly spooky behavior of the young woman he has been sent to guard, who wanders the halls in a zombielike state, claiming to have murdered people and to have seen the devil.

The temple and all that goes on there—or appears to go on—is a wonderful metaphor (and Hammett, evidently sensing this, is said to have greatly expanded its role and introduced it much earlier in the hardcover version of the tale) for the novel's theme: the exploitation of the need to believe. Even the curse wished on her by her dying stepmother—a continuation of the larger curse said to control the destiny of all the Dains—is embraced by poor Gabrielle, and continually urged on the bewildered detective, because at least it "explains" the monstrous series of events that seem to dog her life.

Indeed, for all the Op's casual dismissal of it as little more than "words in an angry woman's mouth," the curse seems to be slowly, relentlessly fulfilled as a series of persons close to Gabrielle one by one turn up dead under a variety of strange and often downright sinister circumstances. And the remaining threads of sanity she clings to are progressively severed as she surrenders to the morbid mysteries of the cult and the gathering darkness of despair.

But just as the Op takes obvious pleasure in exposing the temple's fakery, Hammett dispels the magical gloom that pervades the story with the hard edge of his realism. Most of Gabrielle's spooky behavior, not to mention her highly suggestible disposition, is inspired it turns out by nothing more spiritual than "a skinful of hop"—first cocaine, then morphine. Her drug habit and eventual "cold-turkey" cure at the hands of the Op are described with the clinical eye of one who had, in the employ of Pinkerton's no doubt, known his share of "hopheads" and probably seen at least one kick the habit: the attacks of sneezing and yawning, the painful sharpening of the senses as the body's system throws off its anesthetizing cargo of poison, followed by the lump in the throat and the aching in the jaws and the hollows behind the knees that signal the approach of the ordeal's end (not to mention the diminished sex drive of an addict, which plays a part in the story).

The compelling power of other popular beliefs is similarly

dispelled. It is "as foolish to try to read character from the shape of ears," the Op tells Gabrielle, "as from the position of stars, tea-leaves, or spit in the sand," and "anybody who started hunting for evidence of insanity in himself would certain find plenty, because all but stupid minds [are] jumbled affairs." The "sinister" blacks and Mexican who seem at first to have some involvement in the dark work afoot turn out to be loyal servants whose "strange" ways have merely cloaked their essential innocence. Small-town law-enforcement officers bicker and covet one another's wives, men and women act in precipitous and often thoughtless ways—motivated by such eternal principles as jealousy, rage, lust and fear of exposure.

But mostly lust.

More than five decades of detective fiction, movies and television shows later, it is easy to miss the revolutionary character of Hammett's innovation in the area of motive. Gone are the bloodless villains of earlier detective fiction, monsters of greed or some vague compulsion to indulge in sly games of one-upmanship with the police. Hammett's villains—indeed the "good" characters sometimes seem to differ from the "bad" ones only in degree—are real twentieth-century adults, as earthy and lust-ridden as those in any soap opera. There "was nothing to show that her influence on people was any worse than anybody else's," the Op says of his attempt to convince Gabrielle of her normality, "it being doubtful that many people had a very good influence on those of the opposite sex." Fitzstephan may possess the elephantine ego of a Moriarity, but his rage is based on something as pedestrian—and human—as wanting a woman he cannot have.

Modern social realities such as adultery and drugs had never played so intimate a part of anyone's detective fiction—the great Sherlock's much-vaunted cocaine habit notwithstanding—as they do in Samuel Dashiell Hammett's second novel.

Oddly, it is in this novel—which Ernest Hemingway pronounced Hammett's "bloodiest to date"—that his detective hero is at his saintliest. After the agonizing self-doubts of *Red Harvest*, *The Dain Curse* shows the Op to be more clearly than ever on the side of the good. And it is Hammett's choice, oddly enough, of a vulnerable young woman—more genuinely innocent than any other he had created—that allows the hard-bitten Op to escape the old pattern to which he so often succumbs in the earlier stories. His hard-boiled patter is at its most transparent, his idealism the least camouflaged. And though he protests to Gabrielle that he is "only a hired man with only a hired man's interest in your troubles," the reader doesn't believe him for a moment. The Op even seems, in the last line of the story (which turns characteristically on himself), to enjoy the idea that he might have had, as he kiddingly understates it, "a refining influence" on the young lady.

"Do I believe you because you're sincere?" she asks the Op at one point, introducing a favorite theme of Hammett's (and one particularly at issue in this book). "Or because you've learned how—as a trick of your business—to make people believe in you?" "Your belief in me is built on mine in you," the Op answers her kindly. "If mine's unjustified, so is yours. So let me ask you a question first: Were you lying when you said, 'I don't want to be evil'?" "Belief" is a word that crops up often in the course of this novel. And it is her belief in him, as the Op understands only too well, that will be the key to her recovery from years of addiction.

Is it love, mere sentimentality—or something else—that motivates the Op to lead her to her cure and to stick with her through her arduous journey back from the depths of hell? Hammett avoids a straight answer. "I'm twice your age, sister; an old man," the Op barks in answer to her question. "I'm damned if I'll make a chump of myself by telling you why I did it, why it was neither revolting nor disgusting, why I'd do it again and be glad of the chance."

But a clue may lie in the next sentence out of his mouth, which chides her about parading around with her robe "hanging open." ("You ex-hopheads have to be careful about catching cold," he quickly adds, undercutting the moment again with a piece of Hammett's interesting clinical information.) But it would be unfair to suggest that his interest in her is merely carnal—though Hammett further teases us, a few pages later, when she suddenly decides he's "a monster. A nice one, an especially nice one to have around when you're in trouble, but a monster just the same, without any human foolishness like love in him, and—What's the matter? Have I said something I shouldn't?" (What has she seen—a sudden tear? a look?) After which he indirectly admits—in seriousness? in jest?— that he is drawn to her even as the monster Fitzstephan was. "Oh, dear!" is all Gabrielle can say. Though in what tone of voice we can only guess.

As a novel, *The Dain Curse* has its weaknesses. Though Hammett is said to have heavily reworked the magazine material in preparing the book version and to have made many striking improvements, there is something less satisfying about the book's structure than, say, that of *Red Harvest*. The wonderfully vivid temple setting is confined almost entirely to the second quarter of the book, which subsequently jumps back and forth between the dusty gulches of the southern California coast and some fairly colorless rooms somewhere in San Francisco. Most disappointingly, the book is overly talky: We are told in the last pages—in a utilitarian kind of shorthand style—much concerning the lives of these characters that a traditional novelist would have found better ways to show.

But the story's logic is airtight, and its characters true. There are no clumsy distortions or maddening false clues such as mar many a mystery novel. No jejune switches in point of view in order to make the mystery work—such as spoil Agatha Christie's overpraised story, "Three Blind Mice" (later adapted for the stage as *The Mousetrap*), in which one moment we are inside a character's head, privy to her most intimate thoughts, and the next are not even allowed to see the mysterious person she is talking to, though we can *hear* his voice! *The Dain Curse,* by comparison, is most artfully managed. And the variations worked on the novel's theme—the exploitation of the need to believe—are positively brilliant. For just as her cruel stepmother's version (later cast in doubt) of how Gabrielle's mother died drove the gullible girl into the unprincipled clutches of the Haldorns, who further exploited her belief in her own evil and in the operation of some sinister force in her life, so Gabrielle's ultimate deliverance was made possible by her belief that the detective sought only her good and would stand by her. But the last and most perfect stroke is the diabolical twist worked on the book's theme—a turn worthy of Fitzstephan—in its final pages.

Turned into the mangled wreck of a human being by a homemade bomb—he has lost his right arm and leg and at least half of his face—Fitzstephan had in some ways received a fitting punishment for his sins. (The shock of this development is all the greater coming as it does at a point when all but the canniest of readers must still believe in the good-natured innocence of Fitzstephan.) But the Op's—and presumably Hammett's—deeper sense of justice demanded some worse fate still for the evil genius who had brought so much misery into so many lives.

The Op finds the answer in belief. Or, to be more precise, in the exploitation of Fitzstephan's need to believe that he has succeeded in pulling off a monstrous joke on the world—having convinced both the jury and the newspapers, through his own brilliant defense, "that nobody but a lunatic" could have committed so many and such heinous crimes, and having as a result gotten off scot free to end his days, such as they are, undisturbed on an island in Puget Sound. (His helpless condition makes it unnecessary that he be kept in a mental hospital.)

The Op simply conveys the impression that he believes Fitzstephan to be actually insane. And testifies to the effect that he considers the novelist "legally entitled" to escape hanging.

> Owen Fitzstephan never spoke to me again. . . . He wanted the rest of the world, or at least the dozen who would represent the world on his jury, to think he had been crazy . . . but he didn't want me to agree with them. As a sane man who, by pretending to be a lunatic, had done as he pleased and escaped punishment, he had a joke—if you wanted to call it that—on the world. But if he was a lunatic who, ignorant of his craziness, thought he was pretending to be a lunatic, then the joke—if you wanted to call it that—was on him. And my having such a joke on him was more than his egotism could stomach.

Hammett's own ego was getting a good deal of stroking. Between the appearance of the last installment of *Red Harvest* in February 1928 and the final installment of *The Dain Curse* in February 1929, the circulation of *Black Mask* had increased, writes William F. Nolan, by 30,000. Hammett was in demand. And with the publication in book form of *The Dain Curse* later in the same year his fame with an ever-growing public seemed assured.

But the popular Continental Op, that new kind of detective hero who had so captured the public's imagination, would appear in only three more stories. Hammett had outgrown him, and the possibilities the series presented. His next novel, which was to unfold in the pages of *Black Mask* over five consecutive months beginning that September, would push the detective genre to heretofore unimagined limits. Indeed, the esteemed critic Alexander Woollcott would pronounce *The Maltese Falcon* "the best detective story America has yet produced." And to do what he had in mind, Hammett needed a new and rather different character.

8
The Wages of Commitment:
The Maltese Falcon
The Glass Key

"I won't because all of me wants to—wants to say to hell
with the consequences and do it. . . ."

Sam Spade to Brigid O'Shaughnessy
in The Maltese Falcon

"Samuel Spade's jaw was long and bony," begins the opening
chapter of what would become Hammett's most famous book,

> his chin a jutting v under the more flexible v of his mouth. His nostrils
> curved back to make another, smaller v. His yellow-grey eyes were
> horizontal. The *v motif* was picked up again by thickish brows rising
> outward from twin creases above a hooked nose, and his pale brown
> hair grew down—from high flat temples—in a point on his forehead.
> He looked rather pleasantly like a blond Satan. He said to Effie Perine:
> "Yes, Sweetheart?"

How fitting, after six years of stories and novels featuring a
nameless hero, that the first two words of Hammett's new book
should be the name of his detective. In the twinkling of an eye the
author is on new ground. The very first thing said about Spade—that
his "jaw was long and bony"—establishes him as the physical
antithesis of the Op, even as it fastens on his most distinctive

feature. There will be repeated references, in the course of the book, to Spade's "wolfish" grin, his characteristic smile that exposes his "eye-tooth" (the upper canine) or his "jaw-teeth," and the unsettling "animal sound" he makes in his throat when he is angry. He is given to "growling" and watching his enemies with implacable "yellowish" eyes.

Even this first brief description is marked by menacing associations. His very name suggests both the gravedigger's implement and the playing card that symbolizes death. He is even compared to the devil himself—but with a paradoxical twist calculated to make us uneasy. "He looked rather pleasantly," says Hammett, "like a blond Satan."

Gone is the ready sympathy for the basically decent, comfortably rounded Op. Spade is all angles (and "quite six feet tall," we are shortly told). He smokes Bull Durham, instead of Fatimas, and rolls his own. He even talks differently. Where the Op might have referred to the woman waiting in his outer office as a client, to Spade she is "a customer." And one cannot imagine the Op saying "Shoo her in, darling. Shoo her in." In Spade's first two or three utterances the reader senses a quality of raw playfulness and the suggestion of a ladies' man quite foreign to the Op. Indeed, Spade's opportunism, his cold businesslike way and his peculiar brand of vulnerability to both women and money—the qualities on which the entire novel will turn—are hinted at here and clearly shown in the course of that first chapter. "We didn't exactly believe your story," he will later tell his stunned "customer" of their first encounter. "We believed your two hundred dollars."

The "we" refers to Spade and his partner, Miles Archer. Gone is the larger support structure of the Op's Continental Detective Agency with its scores of fellow agents only a phone call away when a job gets too big for one man to handle. Gone is the Old Man watching over the comings and goings of his younger agents, a figure whose blessing they seek and whose disapprobation they dread. For the Op, hard and world-weary but still looking up to his own version of a stern father figure, was a projection of a young Pinkerton man's experiences. Spade is the creation of an older Hammett.

He is the quintessential loner. Within weeks after he went into partnership with Archer, he admits later in the book, he was sorry.

The man got on his nerves. And when Archer is killed tailing a man on behalf of their "customer" near the beginning of the book, Spade perfunctorily instructs his receptionist and Girl Friday Effie Perine to have their two names taken off the door and his own put on. It seems unlikely Spade will ever find a partner he wants to go into business with. He is too "high-handed," too given to being "wild and unpredictable," too distrustful finally to be tied comfortably to such an arrangement. He has never even been able to sustain a relationship with a woman, we are later told, beyond a few months.

It is fitting then that the reader enters his life at the very moment that Brigid O'Shaughnessy comes into it. "Shoo her in, darling. Shoo her in," Spade tells Effie, little realizing what he beckons. Within pages his partner is dead, their client has disappeared, and Spade himself is a suspect, caught up in a web of intrigue and murder he does not understand. The rapid series of twists and turns this highly charged plot takes in just the first few chapters is deftly managed as we—and Spade—are swept with a wonderful swiftness into the deadly game under way. It involves a storied statuette—a falcon encrusted with priceless jewels and painted black to disguise its worth—that has been pursued for its possession from Constantinople to Hong Kong by a ruthless band of rivals. Offered money beyond his wildest dreams to retrieve the bird (the whereabouts of which one of the others believes Brigid knows), Spade himself is drawn into the frenzied game of cat and mouse, even as his relationship with Brigid O'Shaughnessy deepens into something very like love. The night they go to bed together, he gets up, while she still sleeps, takes her key and searches her apartment (with a thoroughness only a real ex-detective like Hammett could have described—right down to draining the tank of her water closet).

It is probably next to impossible for anyone who has ever seen the 1941 movie version of *The Maltese Falcon* (starring Humphrey Bogart, Mary Astor, Peter Lorre and Sydney Greenstreet) to read Hammett's novel now without hearing the voices of Bogart and the others delivering the lines. The astonishing thing is how vividly— and distinctively—those characters are already there in Hammett's prose. The obese Caspar Gutman, who lusts for the black bird, is already Greenstreet's characterization of him.

> As he advanced to meet Spade all his bulbs rose and shook and fell separately with each step, in the manner of clustered soap-bubbles. . . . His eyes, made small by fat puffs around them, were dark and sleek. . . . His voice was a throaty purr. "Ah, Mr. Spade," he said with enthusiasm and held out his hand like a fat pink star.

Even the "throbbing" quality of Mary Astor's voice is there in Hammett's description of Brigid. The eyes of the dark Levantine Joel Cairo (a descendant of Hammett's shifty foreigners) dart nervously to nowhere in particular like Lorre's. And Hammett's descrition of Spade's facial expressions seems to anticipate Bogart's. ("The looseness of his lower lip and the droop of his eyelids combined with the v's in his face to make a grin lewd as a satyr's.")

In fact a great deal of emphasis is put on faces and eyes—as in the scene in which Cairo is questioned by the police in Spade's presence.

> When he lifted his eyes they were shy and wary. . . .
> "Try telling the facts," [Lieutenant] Dundy suggested.
> "The facts?" Cairo's eyes fidgetted, though their gaze did not actually leave the lieutenant's. . . . Cairo cleared his throat and looked nervously around the room, not into the eyes of anyone there.
> Dundy blew breath through his nose in a puff that was not quite a snort and said: "Get your hats."
> Cairo's eyes, holding worry and a question, met Spade's mocking gaze. Spade winked at him and sat on the arm of a padded rocker. . . .
> Dundy's hard square face darkened the least of shades. He repeated peremptorily: "Get your hats."

Indeed the most remarkable thing about this suspenseful and complex tale is how much of it is played out in silence—or, to be more precise, in the silences between the hard-bitten dialogue. Such a scene in Hammett's hands becomes almost a ballet of faces:

> Spade turned his grin on the Lieutenant, squirmed into a more comfortable position on the chair-arm, and asked lazily: "Don't you know when you're being kidded?"
> [Police detective] Tom Polhaus' face became red and shiny. Dundy's face, still darkening, was immobile. . . .
> Spade rose and put his hands in his trouser-pockets. He stood erect so he might look that much further down at the Lieutenant. His grin was a taunt and self certainty spoke in every line of his posture.

There is another feature of this passage which is worth noting, though it is something that might at first not seem very important. It is told in the third person, as is the entire novel. Spade does not, like the Op, narrate his own story. Instead he is only another character, albeit the central one, in it. In fact the reader goes nowhere Spade does not go and sees nothing that Spade does not see, though he does not go everywhere Spade goes or necessarily see everything he sees. And he is never once allowed to know what Spade is thinking or feeling. Which leaves the reader just as much in the dark as everybody else with regard to his motives.

That Hammett would suddenly and deliberately, after several years of writing detective stories in the first person, decide to switch to a mode so severely restricted as this raises interesting questions. Was he perhaps intrigued by the idea of studying a detective the way the Op studied other characters? Or by the idea of writing a detective story in which the possibility of the detective's death exists? (It suddenly hits home when Spade is drugged and kicked in the temple by his bitterest enemy that he *can* die, since he is not narrating the story, and is perhaps, given Spade's at times frighteningly realistic universe, destined for some violent ending before the last page of the book.) Or was it simply that the story he wanted to write would have been spoiled if we had been even indirectly assured of the essential decency of his main character, who just happens in this case to be a detective? (Else why have gone to such pains to establish from the very first pages that he is not the Op?) The answer is very likely all of the above.

But the key element here is that the voice of Hammett's narrator is strictly neutral, no speaker at all, but an objective, totally impartial voice that betrays not the slightest hint of affection or adulation concerning the detective hero. It is a voice that does not care whether Spade lives or dies, whether good triumphs in the end, or even whether the reader is impressed or exasperated by the main character's actions. And as such it is a logical extension of Hammett's earlier break with the popular conventions of his day.

By adopting the straightforward first-person narrative of the Op Hammett had consciously rejected the hagiographical tradition of detective-story narration stretching from Arthur Conan Doyle to S. S. Van Dine—in which the exploits of the detective hero are recounted in an awed, often abjectly admiring tone by a Watson figure. The great humorist Stephen A. Leacock parodied the tradition with savage irreverence in his story, "The Great Detective":

> "But how," I exclaimed, "how in the name of all that is incomprehensible, are you able to aver that the criminal wore rubbers?"
> My friend smiled quietly.
> "You observe," he said, "that patch of fresh mud about ten feet square in front of the door of the house. If you would look, you will see that it has been freshly walked over by a man with rubbers on."
> "What a fool I was!" I exclaimed, "but at least tell me how you were able to know the length of the criminal's foot?"
> My friend smiled again, the same inscrutable smile.
> "By measuring the print of the rubber," he answered quietly. . . .
> "Idiot that I am," I cried, "it all seems so plain when you explain it."

This grand tradition, which is not without its charm, flourished at least until the death of Rex Stout in 1975 in the popular Nero Wolfe series, though there the inevitable element of hero worship is slyly undercut by narrator/assistant Archie Goodwin's irreverent style, which recalls, as does the series in so many other ways, Boswell's sometimes mischievous manipulation of his hero, Dr. Johnson. Letting the Op tell his own stories enabled Hammett to escape the predictable, smug clichés of what he liked to call the "little-did-he-realize" style.

With *The Maltese Falcon*, he returned to the third person, while preserving the same clear-eyed objectivity he had brought into the genre six years earlier. The result was a morally ambiguous protagonist whose goodness is not presupposed from the start—and a story rich in complications of a very adult and realistic sort. Spade has even slept, the reader learns, with his partner's wife, whose facial prettiness (the faceless narrator informs us with chilling objectivity) "was perhaps five years past its best moment." And when he and Brigid embrace for the first time—a steamy, erotic tableau in which she "put her open mouth hard against his mouth, her body flat against his body" while one of Spade's hands cradles her head, "its fingers half lost among red hair, [the other] hand moving groping fingers over her slim back"—Spade's eyes "burned yellowly" (a

detail the reader cannot imagine he himself shares as a narrator).
Who can say with any certainty what this man is capable of?

At times he seems more soldier of fortune out to snatch his own
gain from the jaws of opportunity than detective trying to solve a
crime, let alone bring somebody to justice. He first accepts a
retainer from Brigid, then another from Cairo. When Gutman confronts him with this potential conflict of interest and tries to establish
who Spade has decided to represent in the "business" at hand, the
answer is disconcerting. "It will be one or the other?" Gutman asks.

> "I didn't say that."
> The fat man's eyes glistened. His voice sank to a throaty whisper
> asking: "Who else is there?"
> Spade pointed his cigar at his own chest. "There's me," he said.

When the falcon turns out to be a fake, Spade delivers them all
into the hands of the police and turns in as a "bribe" the paltry
thousand-dollar bill he has taken from the fat man, insisting merrily
that he has only been "stringing Gutman," can the reader believe
him with any real certainty? "Don't be too sure I'm as crooked as
I'm supposed to be," he tells Brigid when she wonders the same
thing. "That kind of reputation may be good business—bringing in
high-priced jobs and making it easier to deal with the enemy."

As a tactic—if that is what it was—Spade's greed was a master
stroke given the enemy in question. "I do like a man that tells you
right out he's looking out for himself," Gutman purrs in reponse to
Spade's "candor." "I don't trust a man that says he's not. And the
man that's telling the truth when he says he's not I distrust most of
all, because he's an ass that's going contrary to the laws of nature."

Gutman's use of the word *trust* may be the tip-off to what Spade
is up to. The word has turned up like a leitmotif throughout a story
riddled with double crosses and broken promises—between married
people, lovers, enemies, even "businesslike" partners in crime. "I
do trust you," Brigid tells Spade "earnestly" in the first chapter. But
she is lying at that very moment about the facts of the case. She has
not even told him her real name. And when Spade confronts her
with her lies a few pages later she launches into an outburst of
contrition and pleading, using the word *trust* seven times in the

space of nine sentences (though even now she has not told him the whole truth and will continue to deceive and exploit Spade until the very last pages of the book). In fact a rough count reveals that some form of the word *trust* appears no fewer than thirty times in the course of the novel. Not to mention all of the conversations using synonyms for trust that take place between virtually all of the book's characters at one time or another ("I came here in good faith," says Cairo, moments before he pulls a gun on Spade. "I began to be afraid that Joe wouldn't play fair with me, so—so I asked Floyd Thursby to help me," says Brigid). Gutman offers Spade a choice of an "immediate fifty thousand dollars" upon delivery of the bird "or a vastly greater sum within, say, a couple of months." Spade takes a swallow of his drink, for that of course would involve trust.

But the issue especially plagues the painful relationship of Spade and Brigid. When he kisses her, it is with his eyes open. And when, in the last moments of the story, he is listing the reasons why he cannot let her go, the fifth one he gives is that "I've no reason in God's world to think I can trust you and if I did this and got away with it you'd have something on me that you could use whenever you happened to want to."

Some of Hammett's leftist friends may have seen *The Maltese Falcon* as a fable about the capitalist lust for property (such an article, says Gutman, "is clearly the property of whoever can get hold of it," and Spade's own fingers caressing the bird are said to have "ownership in their curving"), others as a parable about the virtue of selfishness or survival of the fittest. But these conversations suggest a more human theme. For Hammett, the whole fabric of society is predicated on trust—"You know I'm willing to go all the way with you all the time," the hotel detective at the Belvedere tells Spade, sharing a piece of information, "But I got a hunch you ain't going all the way with me. What's the honest-to-God on this guy, Sam?"—and not even the simplest of relationships is possible without it.

The first time Brigid O'Shaughnessy ever visits his apartment, Spade is moved to tell her a strange story—a story which held some important meaning for him—which she did not understand. It is about a man named Flitcraft who walked out on his family suddenly one day, without any warning or apparently any premeditation. A beam falling from an office building came within inches of killing him, Spade tells Brigid.

> "He had been raised [to think of life as] a clean orderly sane responsible affair. Now a falling beam had shown him that life was fundamentally none of these things. He, the good citizen-husband-father . . . knew then that men . . . lived only while blind chance spared them. It was not primarily the injustice of it that disturbed him: he accepted that after the first shock. What disturbed him was the discovery that in sensibly ordering his affairs he had got out of step, and not into step, with life."

And so he became, as Spade has become, a kind of existentialist hero cut adrift from the usual certainties that sustain other people— only to settle down with another woman into a life of afternoon golf and bridge games very much like the one he had left. "I don't think he even knew he had settled back naturally into the same groove he had jumped out of in Tacoma," says Spade, "But that's the part of it I always liked."

Even more than the Op, Spade is the poker player at life, bluffing his way through desperate situations and playing his enemies off against one another with the wily art of a born survivor (even his name suggests the gamester). He lives fast and recklessly, sizing up his chances, boldly making his moves. But he has no illusions either about the parameters of his own existence. "I know what I'm talking about," he tells Gutman with a face gone suddenly "dull and lumpy." "This is my city and my game. I could manage to land on my feet—sure—this time, but the next time I tried to put over a fast one they'd stop me so fast I'd swallow my teeth. Hell with that. You birds'll be in New York or Constantinople or some place else. I'm in business here."

Whether he is only "stringing" Gutman here or not, Spade's rejection of Brigid's pleading that he not send her to prison or the gallows (she is guilty of at least one utterly cold-blooded murder) comes down finally, after he has rattled off six or seven other reasons, to his awareness of his own vulnerability. "I won't," he finally shouts at her in the full throes of his agony, "because all of me wants to—wants to say to hell with the consequences and do it— and because—God damn you—you've counted on that with me the same as you counted on that with the others." As the novel nears its conclusion we glimpse the animal in Spade again, looking "hungrily from her hair to her feet and up to her eyes again." But he denies his hunger, knowing that to satisfy it would be his undoing. The scene is infinitely more intense and painful than the parallel one Hammett imagined six years earlier between the Op and Elvira sitting in a parked car by the roadside.

The focus of the movie's ending is on the falcon and the capacity of human beings to delude themselves. "What's that?" asks Effie, looking at the fake falcon. "The stuff that dreams are made of," quips Spade, quoting from Shakespeare's *The Tempest*. (The line does not appear in the book.) The novel ends, much more poignantly, with Spade himself returning to the grim realities of his workaday life. Effie tells him his partner's widow is waiting in the outer office. The symbol of an affair that has long ended. A woman he does not love who wants to marry him. Spade "shivered," writes Hammett. He tells Effie to "send her in"—echoing the words with which he welcomed Brigid O'Shaughnessy and the unknown into his life two hundred and some pages earlier.

He will survive, the reader knows now, and hang onto who he is in the process—whatever happens. It is the process itself that makes his life bearable.

Hammett himself had never been so hard at work. With three acclaimed novels under his belt in just over two years, one might have thought he had earned the right to a vacation. But there were, as always, the exigencies of making a living, and he was making hay while the sun shone. For the past couple of years he had been reviewing occasional books—what else but murder mysteries?—for *The Saturday Review of Literature*. In the spring of 1930 he began reviewing for the *New York Evening Post*—twenty-eight books between early April and the end of June alone. Among them was the newest adventure of S. S. Van Dine's intrepid patrician detective Philo Vance, *The Scarab Murder Case*, with which Hammett had, as might be expected, a field day. He found its ending "not altogether convincing," its effete hero full of "irrelevant profundities" and its police inspectors "as incomparably inefficient, amazingly ignorant, as ever."

That same month the third installment of his own new novel appeared in *Black Mask*. *The Glass Key* must have been an even greater affront to the creator of Philo Vance than Hammett's scathing reviews, for it violated Van Dine's Sixth Rule of Detective Fiction: It had no detective.

The hero of *The Glass Key* is a gambler named Ned Beaumont. The autobiographical resemblances to Hammett himself, who is reputed to have been a compulsive gambler, have long since been noted. Indeed Beaumont also wears a neatly trimmed mustache (like Hammett's), suffers from periodic coughing spells and drinks a lot (as Hammett was already doing). He is also something of a gentleman, though he is given to a certain amount of self-conscious kidding about it, who can chide a friend about wearing silk socks with tweeds, put away his cigar out of consideration for a lady, and even get away with using a word like *gaucherie*. And when, barely three pages from the end of the book, Hammett tells us that Ned Beaumont casually "lit a cigar, sat down at the piano, and played softly until she returned," it does not come as too much of a surprise.

In short, Ned Beaumont is about as unlike Sam Spade or the Op as one could imagine. In contrast to those two hard-working proletarian heroes, who both find their identity in their work ("I'm a detective and expecting me to run criminals down and then let them go free," Spade tells Brigid, "is like asking a dog to catch a rabbit and let it go"), Beaumont is a man who plays for a living. Craps. The ponies. Whatever he can put a bet on.

When the reader discovers him—hunched over the green dice table of a somewhat shady establishment known as The Log Cabin Club—he has wandered into the corrupt world of city politics. An important election is in the offing. Upon its outcome hangs control of the city and its many lucrative construction contracts—a matter dear to a powerful ward boss named Paul Madvig, the young paterfamilias of the club. Beaumont has been a "hanger-on" and unofficial advisor to Madvig for about a year since the latter rescued him when he was down and out.

The two men are like brothers—warmly argumentative and openly affectionate (recalling the relationship of the Op and the cowboy Milk River); Ned has even taken to calling Paul's mother

"Mom." But as the novel opens Madvig has stubbornly disregarded
Ned's best advice and formed an alliance with a patently vain and
empty-headed old senator named Ralph Henry who is running for
one more term. Madvig, we learn, has lost his heart to the senator's
daughter Janet, though she barely knows he exists, and is determined to marry her—in spite of the bad blood between Madvig and
her brother Taylor, a notorious womanizer who has been taking
advantage of Madvig's own twenty-year-old daughter Opal.

Taylor Henry is found dead not far from the club, and a growing
array of evidence points to Madvig as the murderer. Beaumont
however believes his anguished protests of innocence and, deputized as a special investigator for the district attorney's office,
braves much to save his friend's political neck—even to the point of
infiltrating the mob of an Irish mafioso-type named Shad O'Rory,
who is out to destroy Madvig's credibility and power base and
thereby throw the election to the politicians he owns. Beaumont is
locked in a room several days and beaten cruelly and repeatedly by a
pair of sadistic thugs before he can escape to warn Madvig of the
mob's plans. They intend to destroy him with the help of a newspaper publisher named Mathews.

When young Opal Madvig's worst fears about her father are
confirmed by an editorial intimating his guilt in the murder of her
lover, Ned Beaumont replies with a mini-course in how the system
works and how democracy is subverted: "You know a lot about it,"
he says sarcastically. "Mathews is up to his ears in debt. The State
Central Trust Company holds both mortgages on his plant—on his
house too, for that matter. The State Central belongs to Bill Roan.
Bill Roan is running for the Senate against Henry. Mathews does
what he's told to do and prints what he's told to print."

The novel is an unforgettable portrait of political corruption.
Even Paul Madvig, on whom Beaumont lavishes such touching
loyalty, is profiteering on city sewer contracts and has promised to
spring the brother of one of his cronies (who probably is guilty of a
hit-and-run) as soon as the elections are past. But at least Madvig,
unlike O'Rory, does not kill people.

Or does he? For after all Beaumont has suffered for his sake, he
finally confesses privately to the murder, swearing to Ned that it was
an accident and that he only covered it up because he wanted Janet

Henry "more than I ever wanted anything in my life." At length it comes out that the real culprit was the old senator himself, who struck his son with a heavy cane in a fit of rage while the three men were arguing on a street corner. And he and Madvig had covered it up so as not to hurt the senator's chances for reelection.

When the old man asks to be given a minute alone in his room with his revolver, Beaumont denies him the easy way out. "You'll take what's coming to you," Ned snaps. It is a principle dear to Ned Beaumont, who is himself on a losing streak when the novel opens. (The first sentence—with Hammett's characteristic love of such symbolism—has Ned rolling the dice and crapping out.) At Madvig's suggestion that he "try laying off awhile when you hit one of these sour streaks," Ned says something about taking your punishment and getting it over with. "I can stand anything I've got to stand," he tells Paul. In the locked room, he will drag himself over and over again from his bloody cot and crawl painfully to the door—the way the Op kept getting on the wild bronco in "Corkscrew"—only to be beaten back into unconsciousness by his gleeful captors, who decide he is "a God-damned massacrist." One reason Ned distrusts the senator is that "he's never been licked at anything in his life." When Madvig suggests that that is "one of the best reasons I know for throwing in with him," Ned says earnestly, "It's the very worst."

Hammett's decision to make Ned Beaumont a gambler—and a gambler of this particular bent—a gambler, indeed, who is on a losing streak, is no mere accident of autobiography. For this is a novel very much about winning and losing. So obsessed with winning is the old senator that he first delivers his daughter to Madvig to be assured of his support and then leaves his own son lying dead in a gutter—an act which permanently loses him the love and respect of his daughter. So obsessed with winning the old man's daughter is Paul Madvig, that he loses control of his carefully built network of politicians (who finally turn on him in the face of their own reelection fears) *and* the senator's daughter—whom Ned, so to speak, wins (breaking a long jinx on Hammett's heroes).

And the subtheme of facing what cannot be avoided is given its most poignant expression, not in Ned's heroics, but in a strange dream Janet has the first night he comes to dinner in her father's house. She and Ned are walking in a forest, growing hungrier and hungrier, when they come to a house filled with wonderful things to eat. They find a key under the mat and let themselves in. Ironically, the first time she tells Ned about this dream, she suppresses the real ending. The key, she later confesses, was made of glass and shattered in the lock as the door was opened, releasing hundreds of snakes which swarmed over them.

Of course, the erotic meaning of her dream is obvious enough, in view of the fact that she was at the time supposedly attached to Ned's best friend and therefore would have felt guilt at experiencing sexual desire for Ned (taking the familiar Freudian symbolism of snakes in dreams). But the snakes might also be seen as a symbol of the hideous truth of what happened to her brother, which she felt Ned pursued as fiercely as she, and which, she also sensed, once out in the open might devour them both. It is only after she has faced the truth of her father's guilt that Janet can admit the other part of the dream.

Another irony here is that, for the larger part of the novel, Ned Beaumont is not really trying to find a killer and bring him to justice at all; he is just trying to protect Paul Madvig from his enemies. After all, Beaumont is not a detective; he only gets himself deputized in the first place so he can go after a bookie suspected of Taylor Henry's murder who skipped town with some money Ned had won on a horse.

That Madvig seems—and to some extent proves—unworthy of such fierce loyalty as Ned exhibits only underscores Ned's sense of honor in our eyes. One is put in mind of Sam Spade's celebrated explanation to Brigid O'Shaughnessy near the end of *The Maltese Falcon* of why he set out to avenge Miles Archer's death: "When a man's partner is killed he's supposed to do something about it. It doesn't make any difference what you thought of him. He was your partner and you're supposed to do something about it." (A concept that is hopelessly beyond Brigid's own self-centered pragmatism.) "You're right about my being Paul's friend," Ned tells Janet. "I'm that no matter who he killed." He has nothing but contempt for the petty politicians who desert Paul. In the matter of integrity, Ned Beaumont is cut from the same cloth as the rest of Hammett's heroes.

But the underlying theme the two novels share is not so much the wages of honor—Spade's pious words about his duty to his partner notwithstanding—but the wages of commitment to another human being. It is the tantalizing possibility of a *real* relationship that trembles and reverberates through *Falcon* and provides the real moment of truth for Spade, not his perfunctory and essentially empty relationship with Archer, which he appeals to only in the face of his humiliation and despair over having lost Brigid. Spade and Ned Beaumont have the same need for connection. The difference between them is that Spade can't make that commitment—indeed is spared having to take that scary step by Brigid's villainy—while Ned, a gambler, seizes the opportunity and risks everything on it. Even Paul's dishonesty and lack of trust in Ned, interestingly enough, is not sufficient to outweigh Ned's genuine affection and concern for him. Fittingly, it is Ned who is also able to transfer that willingness to share in someone else's fate to a relationship with a woman, while Spade, paralyzed by his own inability to trust any-one—beginning with himself—ends alone.

It is tempting to see in the progression from *Falcon* to *Glass Key* something like the mellowing of Dashiell Hammett, who was shortly to begin a lifelong relationship with playwright Lillian Hellman. (As a matter of fact, *The Glass Key* is dedicated to Nell Martin, a widowed musician and piano teacher with whom Hammett had gone off to New York to live in 1930, leaving his estranged wife "Jose" in San Francisco—just as Ned Beaumont leaves Paul Mad-vig to go to New York with Janet Henry.) Indeed, Hammett's next book was to feature a married couple. But the painful ambivalence of Hammett's earlier heroes, particularly Sam Spade, regarding sustained intimacy and fidelity seems, nevertheless, to be reflected even in Hammett's and Hellman's subsequent relationship, which vacillated for years between talk of marriage and involvements with other partners. Sadly, though they could never quite let go of each other permanently, the two of them were never quite willing to commit themselves totally either, according to Hellman. Almost as though they feared the key might shatter in the lock.

The Glass Key, written like *The Maltese Falcon* in the third per-son, moves in more casual rhythms than the earlier book. Though there are tense moments excitingly depicted, the tone is on the whole less urgent, less intense. It is peppered with colorful underworld argot and visits to half a dozen Prohibition-era speakeasies—glimpses of a time gone by. (The fact that men wore hats as the rule and not the exception figures prominently in the solving of the crime.)

There is more violence than one finds in *The Maltese Falcon*, which, strangely enough, coming so closely on the heels of the notorious scenes of *Red Harvest* and *The Dain Curse*, actually contains practically none (all of the shootings occur offstage). But Hammett's emphasis, more than ever, is on character and relationships. In fact *The Glass Key* is generally considered the closest thing to a regular novel that Hammett ever wrote.

Actually it is not so much a novel as it is a movie—complete with long shots, close-ups, fade-outs and dissolves in which the words someone is speaking dwindle off as it were into inaudibility—creating the sensation that one is overhearing the story's dialogue. The chapters are subdivided into smaller sections which often break off abruptly—and sometimes begin as abruptly, in a different setting or some hours later without the usual transition or explanation, in a manner very like the "quick cuts" of a film, which has the effect of moving the story along in a very engaging manner.

Hammett combined a great ear for dialogue and a knack for strong visuals with a gift for writing spare "stage directions" that get to the heart of character. And Hollywood was not long in discovering him. He was to spend the next twelve years there, polishing other people's screenplays and grinding out original screen stories and loose adaptations from his own fictions, though his name, perhaps because he seems not to have taken this work very seriously, rarely appeared in the credits.

Roadhouse Nights, a Paramount film loosely based on *Red Harvest* and starring Charlie Ruggles, Helen Morgan and Jimmy Durante was released in 1930. The following year saw the first of three screen versions of *The Maltese Falcon* (a forgettable Warner Brothers vehicle for Bebe Daniels and Ricardo Cortez) and *City Streets*, a Paramount film with Gary Cooper, William Boyd and Paul Lukas based on an original story by Hammett. Warner Brothers remade *The Maltese Falcon* in 1936 as *Satan Met a Lady* (with Bette Davis) before its final and best-known version of 1941 with Bogart and company. *The Glass Key* was made twice by Paramount—in 1935 with George Raft, Edward Arnold, Ray Milland and Claire Dodd and again in 1942 with Alan Ladd, Veronica Lake, William Bendix and Brian Donlevy.

But Hollywood's greatest love affair, where Hammett was concerned, would be with his fifth and final novel, an autumnal but thoroughly beguiling whodunit known as *The Thin Man.*

9
Time's Shadow:
The Thin Man

"Nothing changes more constantly than the past; for the past that influences our lives does not consist of what actually happened, but of what we believe happened."

Gerald White Johnson

Long before *The Godfather* Parts I and II and the much-ballyhooed sequels to *Rocky*, *Superman*, and *Star Wars*, there was *The Thin Man*. Dashiell Hammett's highly successful 1934 detective novel (the only one of his books not to have originated in *Black Mask*) inspired a run of no fewer than six movies: *The Thin Man* (released the same year the novel appeared in its hardcover edition), *After the Thin Man* (1936), *Another Thin Man* (1939), *The Shadow of the Thin Man* (1941), *The Thin Man Goes Home* (1945) and *Song of the Thin Man* (1947)—to say nothing of a radio series and a still later TV series centering on the further adventures of mysterydom's original husband-and-wife team, Nick and Nora Charles.

As sleuths they were a refreshing change of pace from the hard-boiled private eye Hammett himself had introduced a decade before. Their breezy banter and lighthearted way with crime and criminals endeared them to an America caught in the throes of the Depression. Just as John Huston's 1941 remake of *The Maltese Falcon* would create an all but insatiable demand for more movies featuring the team of Sydney Greenstreet and Peter Lorre—who became, in the words of one writer, a sort of Laurel and Hardy of villainy—*The Thin Man* spawned a veritable traffic jam of screen vehicles for the duo of William Powell and Myrna Loy, who became the hottest Hollywood "couple" since Fairbanks and Pickford.

Hammett, who had nothing to do with any of the screenplays, was content to accept a paycheck from Metro-Goldwyn-Meyer for thinking up the story lines for the second and third films. And in early 1937 he sold MGM all rights to the *Thin Man* title and characters, with whom he had become "bored," for $40,000. Other men had no doubt written better books than he, Hammett conceded in a letter to his close friend and sometime paramour Lillian Hellman, but nobody had "ever invented a more insufferably smug pair of characters. They can't take that away from me," quipped Hammett, "even for $40,000."

All this becomes the more interesting in light of the fact that Nick and Nora Charles did not even exist in the first version of the novel. The 18,000-word manuscript, which seems to have been begun sometime in the winter of 1930–31 and abandoned the following May, was a straightforward detective story set in San Francisco and, like *The Glass Key* and *The Maltese Falcon*, told in the third person. Its hero is a private detective named John Guild who sets out to find an elusive inventor who has mysteriously vanished and now stands accused of his secretary's murder. Guild has only his gut feeling that the man is innocent.

Guild is still there in the second version of the book, written two years later, as is the basic premise of the plot. But what a sea change has come over Hammett's story. Guild has been stripped of all his moody mystery and "demoted" to the distinctly secondary role of an earnest, but rather pedestrian police detective assigned to the case. The story has been moved to New York, and someone distinctly different from Sam Spade, Ned Beaumont, or the Op is telling it.

> I was leaning against the bar in a speakeasy on Fifty-second Street, waiting for Nora to finish her Christmas shopping, when a girl got up from the table where she had been sitting with three other people and

came over to me. She was small and blonde, and whether you looked at her face or her body in powder-blue sports clothes, the result was satisfactory. "Aren't you Nick Charles?" she asked.

I said: "Yes."

Can one imagine any of Hammett's earlier protagonists in such a domestic scenario—sitting, *waiting* for a woman, let alone a *wife,* to finish her shopping? Yet (as with Spade's bony jaw and Beaumont's jinxed roll of the dice) this is the first thing Hammett wants to tell us about his new hero. Nick Charles, the reader very quickly learns, is a retired private detective who spends more time worrying about his wife's investments and whether there is ice for his scotch than about the cruel vagaries of the underworld. Nick and Nora go to parties (usually with their broker) and the theater (sometimes walking out in boredom after the first act), lie around drinking (a lot) and exchanging witty quips, and sending out for food to all-night delis. Instead of poker, they play backgammon. Nora puts Bach on the record player or reads aloud to Nick from the newly published memoirs of the great Russian operatic basso Fyodor Chaliapin. They even have a dog named Asta, who makes her first appearance, in that irritable way of canines, by pouncing with her paws on Nick's belly unannounced. Asta is in effect the surrogate child of this childless couple—impulsively intruding herself between her "father" and the attractive young woman she finds him dallying with. Nora is glimpsed "at the other end of the leash"—subtly suggesting, with Hammett's typical and quite masterful indirection, the domestic web in which Nick seems to be rather contentedly entangled.

The charming couple obviously owed its inspiration to the relationship of Hammett and Hellman, whom he had met in the winter of 1930–31 shortly after moving to Hollywood. Hellman was delighted, she tells us in her own memoirs, when Hammett told her she was Nora Charles, less certain how she felt when he added that she "was also the silly girl in the book and the villainess." The novel's new ambiance reflected the lifestyle Hammett, now a successful novelist and well-paid movie scenarist, had found in Hollywood and New York, where the ex-Pinkerton operative now frittered away most of his waking life in partying with a circle of new friends that included S. J. Perelman, William Faulkner, Dorothy Parker and the brilliant pianist/raconteur Oscar Levant (who credits

Hammett with introducing him to the works of the sardonic nine-teenth-century American writer Ambrose Bierce).

When Hammett, in a ferocious burst of self-discipline, finally holed up in a New York hotel on East Fifty-sixth Street run by Nathanael West *(Miss Lonelyhearts, The Day of the Locust)* in September 1932 to pound out the second, completed version of *The Thin Man*, it was understandable that his characters and dialogue should reflect the decadent, devil-may care world he had joined. There is even a piano player impishly named "Levi Oscant" at one of the parties the Charleses attend.

The Charleses, to be fair, are on a holiday in New York. In fact *The Thin Man* is the only one of Hammett's novels to be set conspicuously in historical time—the plot unfolds between Thurs-day, December 22, three days before Christmas, and Saturday, December 31, 1932. But one has the distinct impression their normal life back in San Francisco is not all that different. Nick, we are told, has not worked at his former profession for six years, having retired a year after his marriage when Nora's father died, leaving her "a lumber mill and a narrow gauge railroad and some other things." He repeatedly refuses the exhortations of an old friend, Mimi Wynant Jorgensen, his wife Nora, and others to investigate the murder of a young woman named Julia Wolf, secretary to Mimi's ex-husband Clyde Wynant. Wynant, an eccentric, possibly mad inventor who holds many valuable patents and had gone into hiding allegedly because of the sensitive nature of a new invention he is working on, also importunes Charles to take the case in a series of letters mailed to his attorney, Herbert Macaulay, which also contain autho-rizations for large sums of money to be withdrawn from his bank account.

But none of this pleading has any effect on Nick, who enjoys his carefree new life (he is the embodiment of Hammett's tart reference to himself in a 1934 newspaper interview as a "two-fisted loafer"), sleeping late and limiting his exertion to opening a fresh bottle of scotch. Nick is typically lying in bed when he has his first encounter with the ex-convict, Shep Morelli, who is the number one suspect in the murder. Having tried unsuccessfully to convince the thug he is not working on the case, Nick is finally forced to act by the sudden arrival of the police, who were tipped to Morelli's visit. But where

Sam Spade or the Op might have hurtled themselves into a monumental tussle with the gunman, Nick Charles tosses a pillow at him. In fact about the most violent thing Nick does in the course of the story is wrestle Mimi Jorgensen to the couch when she goes berserk one afternoon.

It is only after he himself has been shot at and wounded that Nick reluctantly agrees to investigate the murder—which he does with a mixture of patrician languor and tough-guy cockiness—not as anyone's hired man but to protect himself from whoever is trying to involve him in this case. And *then*, he does almost no real detective work, leaving all of the legwork and most of the actual investigating to Guild and the rest of the police, with whom he cooperates most amicably. Indeed Nick eventually solves the crime and unravels the whole strange business, almost Philo-Vance-like, without ever once visiting the scene of the crime or inspecting the corpse for himself.

Hammett's genius is that he keeps all of this from turning into a mere S. S. Van Dine novel by continually giving us haunting glimpses of another, far more serious dimension—the world of Chandler's "mean streets" where murder is "an act of infinite cruelty." A gun is not just a literary prop, it is a killing machine as real as the daily paper, a grim reminder of a world Nick Charles— and Dashiell Hammett—have left, quite gratefully, behind them. When Mimi Jorgensen's daughter Dorothy innocently pulls a battered automatic from her coat pocket to show it to Nick, Hammett creates an unforgettable little tableau. Asta the pup, "wagging her tail, jumped happily at it," Nick tells us. "The back of my neck was cold." And a few pages later, when Shep Morelli points another gun "very accurately" at Nick, lying there in his pajamas, Nick tells the reader he "could hear the blood in my ears, and my lips felt swollen."

The scene that immediately follows is classic Hammett—a slow-motion sequence that recalls the gun fired at the Whosis Kid from a car going by in the rain. "Open up. Police," comes a voice from the other side of the door.

> "You son of a bitch," [Morelli] said slowly, almost as if he were sorry for me. He moved his feet the least bit, flattening them against the floor.
>
> A key touched the outer lock. I hit Nora with my left hand, knocking

her down across the room. The pillow I chucked with my right hand at Morelli's gun seemed to have no weight; it drifted slow as a piece of tissue paper. No noise in the world, before or after, was ever as loud as Morelli's gun going off. Something pushed at my left side as I sprawled across the floor.

But this scene, which occurs on page twenty-six, is the only real violence—or action, for that matter—Nick will engage in for the rest of the book. Just as Hammett, after the shocking bloodbaths of his Op novels, wrote a book (*The Maltese Falcon*) in which not a single killing—and very little actual violence—occurs "onstage," now in *The Thin Man* he witholds action itself. Hammett's fondness for understatement, evident in his earliest work, has finally won the day. The final word of the book, "unsatisfactory," curiously echoes Nick's use of the word "satisfactory" on the book's first page— almost as though the two words were meant to frame Nick's laid-back narrative. Nick speaks the one, Nora the other; between them hangs their life together—more of which below.

Others have seen Hammett's final detective novel as merely a "lazy" book. "Unlike Hammett's previous novels in which the detective went hunting evidence, in *The Thin Man* the evidence comes to Nick Charles," writes Richard Layman, charging that "Hammett plotted his novel like a short story then padded it into a novel." To be sure, *The Thin Man* lacks the tense feeling of organization that makes *The Maltese Falcon* such a nail-biter. There is even the odd insertion of a two-thousand-word excerpt from another book—the rather bizarre account of one "Alfred G. Packer, the 'maneater,' who murdered his five companions in the mountains of Colorado, ate their bodies and stole their money" back in the winter of 1874. Even Lillian Hellman told friends she believed the fragment, which has no ostensible connection with the rest of the novel, was simply thrown in to fill pages by a pressured Hammett trying to fulfill an overdue obligation to his publisher. The passage is taken from Maurice Duke's *Celebrated Criminal Cases of America*, which Nick pulls from his bookshelf to amuse Dorothy's inquisitive kid brother Gilbert, a brainy pest who is drawn to morbid subjects like cannibalism. Curiously, this same book was also evidently Sam Spade's favorite bedtime reading: It is the book on which Spade's alarm clock rests at the beginning of Chapter 2 of *The Maltese*

Falcon. But whether or not this is some sort of hard-boiled inside joke of Hammett's, most of his critics have found it difficult to look upon the five-page digression as anything more than an irrelevant piece of self-indulgence in an interesting but flawed book.

Elsewhere in the pages of *The Thin Man*, by curious contrast, Hammett is almost painfully scrupulous in his realism. The reader never hears what is being said on the other end of a phone conversation, for instance, unless it is Nick who is holding the receiver—a subtle touch which makes a great deal of sense. And such glimpses as we are given of the underworld are marked by a crisp and highly satisfying authenticity.

The loveliest touch of all however is the central conceit of the novel itself—a metaphor as fine as any invention of Hammett's mind: the "Thin Man" of the book's title, which refers not to Hammett's dapper hero but to the elusive suspect, the mad inventor Wynant, who reminds one of the police officers of the joke about "the guy who was so thin that he had to stand in the same place twice to cast a shadow." The beauty of the metaphor is of course that Wynant, the reader learns at the end of the book, does not even *exist*—has not existed, in fact, since the very first page of the story, except as a figment of everybody else's imagination—thanks to the clever machinations of the lawyer Herbert Macaulay, who has been composing all of the scientist's supposed correspondence authorizing him to raid his former client's bank account and extensive stock portfolio. Hammett clearly enjoys his conceit enormously. "What's he like?" Nora asks Nick on page nine. "Tall—," says Nick, "over six feet—and one of the thinnest men I've ever seen." One of the thinnest men, indeed. The object of all their obsessions—the figure who sends them all scurrying madly about, racking their brains and adjusting their own perceptions of reality, will turn out to be nothing but a shadow.

Ironically, the "Thin Man" of the title became almost immediately identified with Nick Charles, whose continuing adventures on the silver screen were given titles, in the all-leveling imperative of sequel tradition, such as *The Song of the Thin Man*, *The Thin Man Goes Home*, etc. A similar expediency on the part of Hollywood led to a permanent identification in the mind of the public of the name Frankenstein with the famous monster and not, as Mary Shelley had in mind, with the scientist who created him. But it was actually Alfred Knopf, Hammett's publisher, who seems to have started all the confusion by running a photograph of Hammett himself "as the Thin Man"—obviously meant to be Nick Charles—on the dust jacket of the first edition.

Nevertheless, it is an inescapable fact that this, the most successful of all Hammett's books, is also probably the most seriously flawed, or at least the most disappointing from a purely literary point of view. Though the undeniably likable Charleses may well be, as Lillian Hellman has said elsewhere, "one of the few marriages in modern literature where the man and woman actually like each other and have a fine time together," their relationship is never tested. Unlike every one of Hammett's earlier heroes, Nick is never pushed to any kind of moral crisis. There is no moment of truth in *The Thin Man*.

Set beside Nick, the Op, Ned Beaumont, even the "satanic" Sam Spade (maybe *especially* Spade) are seen as passionate men. Nick is *too* cool, *too* detached, too well insulated from the world of feelings around him. Or maybe it is only that Hammett, for the first time, lacks the stomach (or real interest?) to test Nick's humanity in any serious way. Nick's befriending of poor battered Dorothy over her mother's shrill objections pales in comparison with the Op's devotion to Gabrielle Leggett or Ned Beaumont's fierce loyalty to Paul Madvig. He has even made his detective a Greek—a decision that may take on some significance in the light of a remark Hammett makes about Greeks in one of his earliest published writings, the 1923 magazine piece "From the Memoirs of a Private Detective":

> Of all the nationalities haled into the criminal courts, the Greek is the most difficult to convict. He simply denies everything, no matter how conclusive the proof may be; and nothing so impresses a jury as a bare statement of fact, regardless of the fact's inherent probability or obvious absurdity in the face of overwhelming contrary evidence.

In *The Thin Man* Hammett seems to be having a perverse kind of fun with this idea. "She's got so much confidence in you, Nicky," Nora says feelingly, referring to Mimi Jorgensen. "Everybody trusts Greeks," quips Nick. And a handful of pages later, an exasperated Mimi herself is telling Nick, "You're the damndest evasive man."

This only a few lines before the most explicit and extended discussion yet of Nick's Greek parentage.

> "You like Nick a lot, don't you, Nora?" Dorothy asked.
> "He's an old Greek fool, but I'm used to him."
> "Charles isn't a Greek name."
> "It's Charalambides," I explained. "When the old man came over, the mugg that put him through Ellis Island said Charalambides was too long—too much trouble to write—and whittled it down to Charles. It was all right with the old man; they could have called him X so they let him in."
> Dorothy stared at me. "I never know when you're lying."

But while Nick's "evasiveness" is one of the most disarming things about him, it is also finally one of the most disturbing. He moves through his current world of endless parties and almost automatic banter without ever really engaging anyone on any meaningful level. (None of this admittedly would be much cause for rumination in a detective novel except in the light of Hammett's earlier fiction—in which these are issues that matter very much and are always, at some point, confronted.) He seems to hold even Nora at arm's length, occasionally interacting with her with the same fatherly (read: distancing) affection he shows to the twenty-year-old Dorothy. "Tell me the truth, Nick: have I been too silly?" Nora asks him. He shakes his head. "Just silly enough." Nick, we are told, is forty; Nora is twenty-six. (Hammett was thirty-eight, Hellman twenty-seven when he sat down to write *The Thin Man*.)

But Nick's inability to sustain a serious conversation may go deeper than that. Others have commented on the emptiness of the lives of Hammett's characters in this book, including Nick and Nora. The story unfolds over what is for most Americans the most joyful and sentimental of holidays, yet Nick and Nora's exchanging of Christmas presents is almost perfunctory. The reader has the distinct impression that not even New Year's Eve or the coming of the New Year will evoke any quickening of the spirit in the strangely deadened lives of this superficially charming couple, will prove no occasion at all except for another bout of silly partying and still more drinking. Indeed, there are so many references to his drinking and hangovers in the first pages of the book that by the beginning of Chapter 4 drinking has become almost a subtheme.

> That afternoon I took Asta for a walk, explained to two people that she
> was a Schnauzer and not a cross between a Scottie and an Irish terrier,
> stopped at Jim's for a couple of drinks.

> She scowled at me. "And stop talking to me as if I was still twelve."
> "It's not that," I explained. "I'm getting tight."

> In the next room "Rise and Shine" was coming through the radio. My
> glass was empty.

> I said: "Let's all have a drink."

Offered a drink by Mimi Jorgensen when he drops by her
apartment briefly one night, he accepts, adding, "But you'd better
make it a short one; Nora's waiting downstairs in the cab." The very
first time we ever see Nick, he is sitting alone—drinking.

> I was leaning against the bar in a speakeasy on Fifty-second Street,
> waiting for Nora.

—a detail that might have been unimportant, except for the thematic
importance we have seen Hammett attach to his opening sentences—and the fact that the next morning Nick doesn't want to go
out to meet his old army buddy Herbert Macaulay for lunch because
he is hung over, and that he obviously drinks, by his own admission,
to get drunk. "How do you feel?" Nora asks him the morning after
his encounter with Morelli. "Terrible," Nick replies. "I must have
gone to bed sober." "For God's sake," he says to her on another
occasion, "let's have a drink." Indeed on the very last page of the
novel we find Nick cracking that "This excitement has put us behind
in our drinking."

Of course everybody in this book drinks—even the police—and
seems to pay an inordinate amount of attention to the whole ritual
(these were after all the last days of prohibition, which was repealed
a few months after the novel's publication in book form). But Nick's
preoccupation with alcohol and with getting drunk is so pronounced
that it almost asks for comment. One continually expects Hammett
to confront the issue in some way, but he never does. Nick's
drinking never leads, as it did with the Op in *Red Harvest*, to an
episode of true horror and a powerful crisis of conscience. Only to a
kind of comfortable numbness—which cannot help but remind one
that Hammett himself, who had a lifelong problem with alcoholism,

was already drinking heavily at this time. On "the night we had first met," wrote Hellman years later, "he was getting over a five-day drunk and he was to drink very heavily for the next eighteen years"—until, warned by a doctor that he would kill himself if he didn't stop, Hammett quit cold.

The author gives the distinct impression that Nick Charles is running away from something. And the only thing that seems clear is that it has to do with his past—his other life as a detective. Is it his inability to deal with his current inactivity—the loafer's life he has always thought he wanted—in contrast with the life-or-death excitement, or even just the honest work, of his past? Is the reader seeing Hammett's celebrated proletarian hero, who has been described as the quintessential "job-holder," cut off from the life-giving force of honest labor? Maybe, though Hammett stops just short of bringing the issue to a boil.

But the very point at which this novel becomes the most frustrating is also the point at which it becomes the most fascinating. For Hammett has left what seems to be an ingenious trail of clues so structural in nature as to be nearly subliminal—and from the very first pages of the book. Nick Charles is a man not only cut off from, but *pursued by* his past. Hammett's decision to begin his story at the moment he does is highly significant in this regard. It is the moment in which a person from Nick's past—more specifically, from his *old* life—suddenly enters his new life, bringing with her a whole network of old entanglements: an old affair with her mother, Mimi Wynant Jorgensen, an old case of Nick's which was never solved, and the whole cast of characters connected with it . . . the past, in short, as unfinished business. Indeed Mimi's new husband—who seems for so long to be the one new character in the drama—turns out to be Clyde Wynant's old nemesis. "A fellow who'd worked for him accused him of stealing some kind of invention from him," Nick explains to Nora. "Rosewater was his name. He tried to shake Wynant down by threatening to shoot him, bomb his house, kidnap his children, cut his wife's throat—I don't know what all—if he didn't come across. We never caught him." But the real villain here will turn out to be yet another figure from Nick's past, his old army buddy Macaulay.

The fact that Hammett makes so much of Nick's resisting a

return to his past life as a detective—even as he is sucked into a sinister new plot involving a cast of characters from the life Nick has thought he left behind—suggests we may be on the right track here. Nick has come back "home" to New York on a visit, and his past literally catches up with him. The lesson, if there is a lesson here, seems to be that one must face one's past or be destroyed by it. And on one level, Nick does that.

But there is another theme interwoven with the first. And it has to do with who Nick really is. "Aren't you Nick Charles?" Dorothy asks him on the first page of the novel, coming up to him at the bar. "Yes," Nick unthinkingly answers. But she soon presses her point, one that unsettles him; for she means Nick Charles, *the detective*— an identity Nick has forsaken and keeps insisting is not him anymore. The later reference to his father's original name, Charalambides, is very much to the point: Nick's father had shed an older identity and become someone else. And Nora later calls Nick by that name in an intimate moment, suggesting that he too is someone other than who he pretends to be. Indeed, Nick's reasons for turning his back on his former identity as a detective are not so dissimilar from his father's in sacrificing his old name willingly for the opportunity of gaining admittance to America with all its plenty and its promise of the good life.

The shadow that has fallen over Nick's life is that of time itself: the inescapable past with its uncomfortable echoes of old aspirations and uneasy compromises, its unfinished business and its unanswered questions. One of those questions, says Malcolm Cowley, is frequently, as one grows older, who was I and why did I do what I did and not do certain other things? The difficult part about trying to answer such questions is that one's sense of what actually happened changes. It is in this regard that people out of one's past can be fascinating, in a morbid sort of way, like time travellers bringing news of a forgotten or as yet unknown era.

Dorothy had been "a kid of eleven or twelve" when she had known the old Nick. "I was fascinated by him," she tells Nora, "a real live detective, and used to follow him around making him tell me about his experiences. He told me awful lies, but I believed every word." Her fascination with what she believes to have been the romantic nature of that life is paralleled, interestingly, by Nora's. Just as Dorothy, now twenty, tries to recapture a connection with that past, Nora yearns to see her husband in action as the mythic detective he used to be: "You didn't have to knock me cold," she complains to Nick after the struggle in the bedroom with the armed gangster Shep Morelli. "I knew you'd take him, but I wanted to see it." ("I know bullets bounce off you," she says later in a more tranquil moment, realizing that he has been wounded, "you don't have to prove it to me.")

Aglow with excitement after Nick takes her to a speakeasy run by one Studsy Burke, a mobster he once sent to jail, where she witnesses a scuffle at close range, Nora blurts out impetuously: "I don't understand a thing that was said or a thing that was done. They're marvelous." And a moment later, she playfully confesses: "I love you, Nicky, because you smell nice and know such fascinating people."

Nora even plays at being a detective. And it is great fun. In the last chapter, as Nick finally does his thing, unraveling the whole case with the insight and second-nature methods of a professional, she listens in amazement—and exasperation. "Then you don't know positively that he was robbing Wynant?" she interrupts at one point. "Sure we know," says Nick. "It doesn't click any other way." "Then you're not sure he—" she blurts out at another point. "Stop saying that. Of course we're sure. That's the only way it clicks," says Nick. "But this is just a theory, isn't it?" she interjects a moment later. "Call it any name you like. It's good enough for me," says Nick.

"But I thought everybody was supposed to be considered innocent until they were proved guilty and if there was any reasonable doubt, they—" objects Nora. "That's for juries, not detectives," Nick tells her, followed by a thumbnail dissertation on the way real detectives work:

> You find the guy you think did the murder and you slam him in the can and let everybody you know think he's guilty and put his picture all over the newspapers, and the District Attorney builds up the best theory he can on what information you've got and meanwhile you pick up additional details here and there, and people who recognize his

picture in the paper—as well as people who'd think he was innocent if you hadn't arrested him—come in and tell you things about him and presently you've got him sitting on the electric chair.

It comes down to a question, says Nick, of what you choose to believe—because the facts don't "make any sense otherwise." The problem of *belief* runs throughout *The Thin Man*. In fact the word itself crops up constantly.

"He told me awful lies, but I believed every word."

I believed in her bewilderment, though both it and my belief in it surprised me.

"I don't believe it," she said. "You made it up. There aren't any people like that."

". . . as long as she can get anybody to believe in it. And you, of all people, to be fooled, you who are afraid to believe that—well—that I, for instance, am ever telling the truth."

"This doesn't have to've happened," I reminded him. "It's what Gil says happened."

In fact it is Nick's inability to *believe* in the motives implied in Wynant's "letters"—a kind of "tenth clue"—that drives him to suspect there is something fishy in the whole setup.

This thematic concern may even explain Hammett's inclusion of the strange "Alfred G. Packer" digression. Young Gilbert, like us, is "disappointed in the story I had given him." "It's very interesting, but, if you know what I mean, it's not a pathological case," says Gilbert, who has evidently decided to dismiss Packer's own later admission that he had, subsequent to murdering the first of his snowbound companions, grown "fond" of human flesh. "It was more a matter of that or starving," reasons Gilbert, rejecting the episode as a case of true cannibalism. "Not unless you want to *believe* him," says Nick simply (italics mine).

Hammett has moved, in the course of his five novels, from the Op's compulsive litanies rehearsing all the possible scenarios of what really happened . . . to juxtaposing various characters' *versions* of what happened. In *The Thin Man*, we have Macaulay's version, what is thought to be Wynant's, then Mimi's, then Jorgensen-Rosewater's, and finally Nick's. Nick might have seen through the tissue of lies sooner, he apologizes, "only I was a bit too willing to believe she"—meaning Mimi—had planted a certain piece of evidence at the scene of Wynant's secretary's murder.

Young Gilbert is constantly asking Nick, in effect: Is all of this *true*? Do such things really go on in the world? Do people really eat other people? What does it *really* feel like to be stabbed? shot? ("You only feel the blow—and with a small-calibre steel-jacketed bullet not much of that—at first," Nick tells him. "The rest comes when the air gets to it"). "Listen: remember those stories you told me? Were they all true?" Dorothy asks Nick at the beginning of the book; but when Nora finally learns at the end of the novel how real detectives work, she finds it "all pretty unsatisfactory."

The American public, on the other hand, found it all quite satisfactory indeed—to Hammett's great profit (he is estimated to have earned nearly one million dollars from the book and its spin-offs) and to his demise as a serious artist. For though Hammett would live for another twenty-seven years, *The Thin Man*, published when he was only thirty-nine, was to be his last novel. Hammett would help develop a highly successful—and seemingly endless—series of films, radio and TV series based on his characters, even collaborate briefly on a comic strip called *Secret Agent X-9* with artist Alex Raymond, the creator of Flash Gordon, but the highly influential series of detective novels begun in 1929 was at an end.

Even as Hellman was finishing her first play, *The Children's Hour*, Hammett was grinding out the story line for the first Thin Man movie sequel, beginning a long and frequently wistful second career of cannibalizing his own work for money. Why he stopped writing books has been the subject of intense speculation for decades. His alcoholism? Perhaps. But that is less an answer than another question. The ease with which he now found himself able to make money—a commodity he reputedly went through like water—without having to work as hard as in the past seems to have been another factor. Some would say he had passed into his "mentor" phase and was now pouring his creative energies into teaching Lillian Hellman how to write and molding her (through the most rigorous coaching) into an important playwright. Others, that he was simply tired of fame, of success American-style, and all the hypocrisy and easy superficiality that went with it—which took away his heart for serious work. But *The Thin Man* itself may offer other important clues, for it stands squarely in the midst of the often exasperating tangle of paradoxes that was Dashiell Hammett.

10
The Murder of Innocence: Hammett's Place

There died a myriad,
And of the best, among them,
For an old bitch gone in the teeth,
For a botched civilization. . . .

Ezra Pound, 1920

There is a sense in which Hammett's last novel, whatever else it may have been, was also his own literary obituary for himself. For if *The Thin Man* is on some level the story of a man who is trying to leave his past behind but still finds himself haunted by it, Hammett found himself in the early thirties in a very similar situation.

Lillian Hellman believed Hammett had been made to feel ashamed of his books—mere detective stories—by the literary crowd they now moved in, especially once her plays began to create interest in New York. Ironically, the fact that he *wrote* detective stories was no doubt one of the very things about Hammett these people found so charming. But he came, Hellman felt, to look down on his own work as somehow less worthwhile than theirs, something unworthy of a writer of his obvious gifts. And yet he found himself unable to make the transition from that material he had once felt so comfortable with to the stuff of regular "literature"—though his life was rich enough with such material.

"I've been in a couple of wars—or at least in the Army while they were going on—and in federal prisons and I had t.b. for seven years and have been married as often as I chose and have had children and grandchildren," Hammett would write in a "serious" novel entitled *Tulip* which was begun shortly after he was released from prison and abandoned in 1953, "and except for one fairly nice but pointless brief story about a lunger going to Tijuana for an afternoon and evening holiday from his hospital near San Diego I've never written a word about any of these things. Why? All I can say is they're not for me. Maybe not yet, maybe not ever. I used to try now and then," says Hammett's narrator, a fifty-seven-year-old blocked writer like himself, out duck hunting with an old army buddy from the Aleutians, who is trying to start a new book, "—and I suppose I tried very hard, the way I tried a lot of things—but they never came out meaning very much to me."

This final, maddening mystery eluded the man who had made a career—in fact two careers—out of solving mysteries. Is it possible that, just as the Op is made to confront in *Red Harvest* the question of what is happening to his humanity, *The Thin Man* was an attempt, perhaps not even fully conscious, on Hammett's part to deal with what had been happening to him? Nick, the reader is told, has quit the detective business to look after his wife's financial interests; by the time he appears he has become quite thoroughly distracted by the family investments, which need constant care and watching over, though they demand a minimum of exertion on his part. Hammett himself had, in a sense, "retired" from the business of serious writing, devoting the better part of his energies now to cultivating Hellman's promise and to looking after his own literary properties. Only reluctantly was he, like Nick, coaxed out of retirement to gratify his fans with one more dazzling performance.

And just as Hellman, the woman in Hammett's life, inspired not only Nora but "also the silly girl in the book [Dorothy] and the villainess [Mimi Jorgensen]," it may be that Hammett lurks not only behind Nick but also the vanished inventor Clyde Wynant, the "Thin Man" of the title. For there was also a sense in which a part of Hammett—someone he had been once, an inventor of ingenious things no one had hitherto imagined—had slipped away while every-one was looking and become little more than an illusion, a ghostly presence barely capable of casting so much as a shadow. For years the radio shows and movies kept up the illusion of his presence; the fact is that by the day in 1951 when *The Adventures of Sam Spade* finally went off the air he had been gone for years.

His publishers may not after all have been so far off the mark: the Thin Man would become a fitting image, more fitting than they could have known, for the aging Hammett—gaunt, mysterious, a stoic, almost ascetic figure who increasingly indulged himself in "rich refusals" until he was little more than skin and bone. By then prison had broken his health and he knew he no longer had the energy to write a real book again—his kind of book—a book like the ones that had captured the imagination and respect of literary figures on both sides of the Atlantic, and had changed forever the landscape and the possibilities of the detective story. "If you are tired you ought to rest, I think," he has the old writer tell the younger man in the *Tulip* fragment, "and not try to fool yourself and your customers with colored bubbles." It is the last sentence in the manuscript.

How much of Hammett is in his books and to what extent they can or ought to be read as a kind of spiritual autobiography of one of the more interesting writers America has produced are questions which must, finally, be left to the biographers. What does fall within our purview here however is the question of Hammett's impact on the genre in which he chose, throughout the peak years of his creativity, to concentrate his efforts so single-mindedly. But to properly appreciate that contribution, it is necessary to look at Hammett's historical position in the development of the detective genre.

The detective story Hammett inherited was a product of nine-teenth-century romanticism. Fittingly, the father of the genre was Edgar Allan Poe (1809–1849). The century-long fascination with the forming of the individual soul, the less-rational levels of human consciousness, the perfectibility of society and the essential loneli-ness of human beings produced a good deal of memorable poetry, along with the novels of Dickens, the Brontë sisters, Melville and Hawthorne. But it was, perhaps most vividly, in the work of Poe that the reading public was introduced to the darker side of that new vision of human nature. Poe's morbid obsession with the evil strain in human beings, and such phenomena as cruelty, crime and re-morse—or the absence of remorse—and madness, found unforgetta-ble expression in such tales as "The Pit and the Pendulum," "The Fall of the House of Usher," "The Mask of the Red Death," "The Cask of Amontillado" and that classic of the guilty conscience—the epitome of the old saw that murder will out—"The Tell-Tale Heart."

Poe's fascination with nightmares and drugs—preoccupations that figure prominently in the work of Dashiell Hammett—goes back to Samuel Taylor Coleridge's experiments with opium and the poetry that resulted. The subject has been thoughtfully explored in such books as M. H. Abrahms's *The Milk of Paradise* and Alethea Hayter's *Opium and the Romantic Imagination*. Indeed the whole tradition of psychological repression in matters of sexuality and other irrational drives which are now virtually synonymous with the Victorian Era also erupted, on the other side of the Atlantic from Poe, in a book like Robert Louis Stevenson's *Dr. Jekyll and Mr. Hyde* (1886) and, eventually, in the work of Sigmund Freud, whose landmark study *The Interpretation of Dreams* (1900) suggested the presence of a Mr. Hyde of sorts down deep inside each one of us. For Charlotte Brontë, it had been a matter of a dark secret from a man's past locked away in the attic of a gloomy mansion, for Poe the corpse of a murdered man hastily buried under the floorboards of his own house—directly beneath the very spot on which the police sit having tea with the tormented murderer.

But if the Victorians were fascinated by the dark logic of the evil personality, they were to become equally fascinated by the uncanny talent, also buried deep within human beings, for unravel-ing those sinister processes. The noble genius of Sherlock Holmes and the evil genius of Moriarity are really just two sides of the same romantic coin.

Holmes—the apotheosis of the romantic belief in the perfecti-bility of human beings, a walking example of the untapped resources of the human psyche—is believed to have been inspired by the detective hero of three of Poe's stories, a perspicacious Frenchman by the name of C. Auguste Dupin. In "The Murders of the Rue Morgue" (1841), "The Mystery of Marie Roget" (1845) and "The

Purloined Letter" (1845)—believed in their turn to have been inspired by the memoirs of Eugène François Vidocq, who opened the world's first detective bureau in Paris in 1817—the brilliant Dupin performs feats of deduction, outshines the bumbling police, amazes his narrator-companion, solves a trio of bizarre mysteries—and single-handedly creates a brand new kind of literature.

The English novelist Wilkie Collins introduced the new genre to his homeland with *The Moonstone* (1868), while a woman, Anna Katharine Green, became the first American detective novelist a decade later with *The Leavenworth Case* (1878); but it was with *A Study in Scarlet* (1887), the first of Sir Arthur Conan Doyle's fictional accounts of the exploits of Sherlock Holmes, that the detective story first reached a mass public. For nearly three decades the genre would be synonymous, in the minds of many people, with the adventures of a brilliant and egoistic citizen sleuth who succeeded where the police had failed—feats usually recounted by a frankly admiring narrator. G. K. Chesterton's wily priest detective made his bow in *The Innocence of Father Brown* (1911); Agatha Christie's arrogant little Belgian Hercule Poirot in *The Mysterious Affair at Styles* (1920); Dorothy Sayers's dashing gentleman scholar Lord Peter Wimsey in *Whose Body?* (1923); Earl Derr Biggers's inscrutable Charlie Chan in *The House Without a Key* (1925) and Willard Huntington Wright's inimitable Philo Vance in *The Benson Murder Case* (1926). And their imitators were myriad.

Sayers's sleuth regaled his readers, in between flushing out villains, with snippets of scholarly erudition and cultural small talk, while Biggers's Chan charmed them with pseudo-Confucianisms ("Bad alibi like dead fish—cannot stand test of time"). Hercule Poirot redefined the word imperious in *Who Killed Roger Ackroyd?* But, beneath their eccentric and highly individualistic exteriors, all of these detective heroes had one thing in common: They were all civilized men dedicated to the time-honored values of civilized society. Vance, his readers were told, was fond of quoting Joseph Fouché's famous line: "C'est plus qu'un crime; c'est une faute" (It's worse than a crime, it's a blunder). Murder in the classic Christie story occurs in the context of civilized society—a group of people pent up in an enclosed space (a house, a railway car) with the knowledge that one of them cares not a fig for the rules of the social

contract. It is this fear of a moral anarchist loose in their midst—
and, what is worse, a dissembling anarchist—that creates the ten-
sion.

Of course, planted deeper still is the old romantic faith that
murder will out, that the better side of humanity will triumph and the
evil in our midst once again be routed—or put safely behind bars—
by some heroic individual. The art of such a story lies in its
fastidious orchestration, the slyly planted clues, the suspicious
characters teasingly moved around like so many chessmen, the
series of startling revelations—all leading with wonderful inevitabil-
ity toward that final dramatic moment of triumph in which our
redoubtable hero rips the mask off the guilty one in a dazzling
display of ratiocination and sheer God-given intuition. When it is
done well, it can be great fun—the fun of tagging along with an
incredibly competent eccentric as he shows up all the graceless
Philistines and plodding "experts"; the fun of trying to beat him to
the punch; the fun of sudden surprises; the fun of seeing the pieces
of an ingenious puzzle slowly assembled.

For some readers, that is enough. The popular mysteries of
S. S. Van Dine (whom two presidents confessed was their favorite
author) set publishing records for detective fiction and inspired,
between 1926 and 1939 no fewer than twenty-seven films. (Indeed,
the year Dashiell Hammett's first novels were published, actor
William Powell, now remembered for the role of Nick Charles, was
busy portraying . . . Philo Vance.) But in the larger realm of fiction it
is difficult to take such stories or their authors very seriously. "How
can you care who committed a murder which has never really been
made to take place, because the writer hasn't any ability of even the
most ordinary kind to make you see or feel it?" the late critic
Edmund Wilson icily observed in his infamous essay, "Who Cares
Who Killed Roger Ackroyd?" "How can you probe the possibilities
of guilt among characters who all seem alike because they are all
simply names on a page?" Such a story, says Wilson, is merely "an
intellectual problem."

In this context one can begin to appreciate the electrifying
impact on the world of the whodunit of the appearance in 1929 of
Dashiell Hammett's *Red Harvest*—followed in rapid succession,
within the space of only two years, by *The Dain Curse*, *The Maltese*

Falcon and *The Glass Key*. Gone were the simplistic formulas, the floor plans of the murder room. Hammett had come, quite simply, out of another tradition—that of the pulps, which had in turn developed out of the swashbuckling melodrama of the dime novels. "The technical basis of the *Black Mask* type of story," wrote Raymond Chandler in *The Simple Art of Murder* (1950), "was that scene outranked plot, in the sense that a good plot was one that made good scenes. The ideal mystery was one you would read if the end was missing. . . . [The] demand was for constant action. . . . When in doubt have a man come through the door with a gun in his hand."

Hammett had also come, moreover, out of the same post-World War I disillusionment that was to produce Ernest Hemingway, Sinclair Lewis, John Dos Passos, James M. Cain, Horace McCoy, Nathanael West and F. Scott Fitzgerald. For many of the sensitive young artists and writers who came to adulthood in the twenties, the unparalleled brutality and slaughter of the Great War, with its nerve gas, tanks and modern artillery, had revealed the sham of what poet Ezra Pound pronounced "a botched civilization" and exposed the world in which they lived as a vicious, dangerous place bereft of any real values and any genuine respect for individual human beings. "Died some, pro patria," wrote Pound of the unspeakable sacrifice of human lives made between 1914 and 1918 and the disillusionment that followed, "non 'dulce' non 'et decor' . . ." (referring to the Roman poet Virgil's famous line proclaiming that it is a sweet and noble thing to die for one's country),

> *walked eye-deep in hell*
> *believing in old men's lies, then unbelieving*
> *came home, home to a lie,*
> *home to many deceits,*
> *home to old lies and new infamy;*
> *usury age-old and age-thick*
> *and liars in public places.*

Many of these writers made little effort to hide their contempt for social and political hypocrisy, as well as for the abuses of international capitalism; some, like Hammett, even explored the alternative systems of socialism or communism. The often cynical manipulation of the working classes by the moneyed interests—even to the point of waging mass war in Europe at the cost of millions of human lives—led, in Hammett's case, to a new brand of villain—from the greedy capitalists of the early stories to the opportunistic politicians and crooked lawyers of his last novels.

The twenties also saw the rise of the trade unions (often in the face of the bitterest opposition from the capitalist class) and a new class-consciousness in America, reflected, as we have seen, in Hammett's stories, most notably in the case of *Red Harvest*. But Hammett was not a one-theme writer or a closet ideologue with a political bone to pick; other developments of the postwar disillusionment also attracted his attention. The rise of pseudoreligious cults in a society which found itself cut off from the comforting realities of the past and no longer "assured," in T. S. Eliot's phrase, "of certain certainties," became the premise for his second novel, *The Dain Curse*. The desperate new materialism and dog-eat-dog pursuit of success and personal fulfillment resulted in *The Maltese Falcon*; and the decadence into which a significant segment of American society increasingly retreated (along with, eventually, Hammett himself) was to become the subject, in many ways, of *The Thin Man*.

"Everything seemed meaningless and unimportant," writes social historian Frederick Lewis Allen of the period. "Well, at least one could toss off a few drinks and get a kick out of physical passion and forget that the world was crumbling. . . . and so the saxophones wailed and the gin-flask went its rounds. . . ."

The frank eroticism of Hammett's novels, a new element in the detective genre, reflects the new permissiveness in sexual matters ushered in with the postwar period. *The Thin Man* was rejected by several magazines as entirely too frank before *Redbook* agreed to publish a somewhat bowdlerized version. The line in which Nora asks Nick if he had an erection while he was wrestling with Mimi Jorgensen was quietly censored. One may glimpse the influence of Freud—whose titillating new theories about sex and the subconscious, says Allen, were being debated over "cocktail-tray and Mah Jong table"—in Nick's explanation of the Wynant-Jorgensen family's extraordinary behavior in terms of repressed libido. "They're all sex-crazy, I think, and it backs up into their heads."

But Hammett's earlier novels were just as shocking, to many

readers, in the new level of violence they introduced to a genre in which murder had hitherto been little more than a necessary intellectual premise for the working out of a clever parlor game. Though Hammett himself had never actually seen any combat in the war, the violence the war had brought home to America was all too apparent to him. A new kind of cynicism, a sense of the cheapness of human life, was in the air. And thanks to the availability of army surplus machine guns and other modern weaponry developed by governments locked in a ferocious struggle for power and influence, the gang wars of the twenties attained a level of firepower hitherto unseen in the streets of American cities. The hardcover edition of Hammett's *Red Harvest* appeared in the same year as the celebrated St. Valentine's Day Massacre. But Hammett did not always need the larger canvas of gang warfare to paint the savagery of his times. He could do it in the look of a man's eyes.

Finally, there was Prohibition. Though America's temperance movement went back to pre-Civil War days, it was the mighty surge of righteousness stirred by the First World War which pushed the Eighteenth Amendment through Congress in the winter of 1917. Ironically, the Great Experiment is now seen as having accelerated the rise of organized crime and the corruption of law-enforcement agencies in the general atmosphere of hypocrisy and profiteering it fostered—realizations not lost on the young Dashiell Hammett. Indeed some might see more than a coincidence in the fact that Hammett's serious writing career ended in the very year in which Prohibition was repealed. The career of the nation's most famous criminal also ended shortly after, on July 22, 1934, the same year *The Thin Man* was published, when the notorious John Dillinger was gunned down by federal agents in front of Chicago's Biograph Theater—an event that, for many, signalled the end of an era.

Fate, in any case, could not have arranged a more perfect close.

But besides his education in the *Black Mask* school of fiction, his political consciousness and a share of the general disillusionment of his generation, Hammett also brought one other new element to the world of detective fiction which his more genteel predecessors and the better known of his contemporary rivals lacked: his experience as an actual detective. Besides a wealth of authentic detail, dialogue bristling with the colorful argot of the underworld of the

twenties and a feel for how real criminals—and real investigators—
think and act, Hammett brought into the detective story the whole
menacing reality of twentieth-century urban crime—the kind his
readers confronted almost daily in the newspapers. Murder, in
Dashiell Hammett's stories, is no longer merely the antisocial impulse of the isolated madman, the arcane villain concocting his
diabolical plots in the privacy of his study, but the direct outgrowth
of life in the modern American city. Hammett had seen in his years
as a Pinkerton detective that most crimes are committed by people
trying to get by, people made desperate by circumstances—or
people, at the other end of the social spectrum, who have so
compromised their humanity in clawing their way to the top that
they will stop at nothing to preserve their holdings.

The point is that for Hammett it was all of a piece—the petty
gunman and the ruthless capitalist, the crooked lawyer and the
ambitious politician. As Ned Beaumont's analysis of how political
corruption is perpetuated suggests, Hammett had no illusions about
the system. This perspective may or may not be found in the
whodunits of some of his contemporaries, but for Hammett it is
always there, at the heart of everything, like a permanent shadow.
He has no illusions. Even his police officers drink bootleg whiskey,
take money from the mob and beat up people.

But they are not the "inefficient boobs" of the Philo Vance
school of detective fiction. At least, not categorically. Sam Spade's
ridicule of Lieutenant Dundy is an act; Spade knows all too well
that Dundy is on to him and will have the facts out on the table in a
matter of time. And in *The Thin Man* police detective John Guild is
smart enough to follow up Nick's half-formed leads; in fact it is the
police, not Charles, who find the body of the murdered scientist and
subsequently track down most of the corroborating evidence needed
to send the conniving lawyer Macaulay to the chair. In the real
world of detection Hammett had known, neither policeman nor
private operative had had a monopoly on shrewd successes—or on
dumb mistakes. In fact Hammett reveals throughout his own books
a healthy respect for what Nick describes to Nora as "ordinary"
routine, though he is also fond of pointing out that all the loose ends
never quite tie up as neatly in life as they do in literature (the faint
traces of blood found on Macaulay's table turn out to be beef blood).

But while Hammett could chide a popular author like S. S. Van Dine (Willard Huntington Wright) for concocting mysteries the authorities "would have cleared up . . . promptly if they had been allowed to follow the most rudimentary police routine," he himself must have maddened the champions of the so-called well-made detective story with his indulgence of another element in his own tales—the element of chance, or, as the Op might have called it, dumb luck. In "Dead Yellow Women" he spots going by in a taxi a suspect who has eluded a fellow operative. Hammett's stories are full of such sudden unexplained twists of fate, though the "breaks" just as often go against his heroes as in their favor. Hammett knows that real life is like that.

"The chief difference between the exceptionally knotty problem confronting the detective of fiction and that facing a real detective," wrote Hammett in "From the Memoirs of a Private Detective," "is that in the former there is usually a paucity of clues, and in the latter altogether too many." In contrast to the all-too-neat, every-peg-falling-into-place summations that were the hallmark of the closing pages of every Agatha Christie whodunit, Hammett's narrators are usually at some pains to remind the reader that certain parts of the big picture they have finally put together are only unprovable supposition. "I always thought," confesses an exasperated Nora Charles, "detectives waited until they had every little detail fixed in—" "And then wonder why the suspects had time to get to the farthest country that has no extradition treaty," Nick snaps. To Nora's frowning objection that "it's not very neat," he retorts: "It's neat enough to send him to the chair . . . and that's all that counts."

In the face of this kind of realism, it was understandable that Hammett should be contemptuous of those who sought to codify the detective story and contain it within structures of a purely literary sport that did not match his own experience or seemed artificially imposed on a genre he obviously felt capable of much more interesting possibilities. He freely violated many of the axioms set forth in S. S. Van Dine's 1928 essay, "Twenty Rules for Writing Detective Stories"—such as No. 6 ("The detective novel must have a detective in it") in *The Glass Key*; No. 7 ("There simply must be a corpse") by constructing *The Thin Man* backwards; No. 12 ("There must be but one culprit, no matter how many murders are committed . . . [so that] the entire indignation of the reader [is] permitted to concentrate on a single black nature") in *Red Harvest*; No. 16 ("A detective novel should contain no long descriptive passages, no literary dallying with side issues") by including the odd digressions in *The Maltese Falcon* and *The Thin Man*; No 17 ("A professional criminal must never be shouldered with the guilt of a crime") and No. 19 ("the motives for all crimes in detective stories should be personal") in "$106,000 Blood Money" and "The Gutting of Couffignal" in which the crimes are committed strictly for money and pretty much by professionals (in fact, Hammett's villains, symptomatic of a society he found altogether too materialistic, often emphasize the "impersonal" nature of their crimes); and No. 3 ("There must be no love interest") in both of the Op novels, *The Glass Key*, and, most disturbingly of all, *The Maltese Falcon*.

To his credit, Van Dine himself was out to rid the genre of certain tired clichés (ennumerated in Rule No. 20) and other unsatisfying abuses of the day. "The problem of the crime must be solved by strictly naturalistic means," he writes in Rule No. 8, "Such methods for learning the truth as slate-writing, ouija-boards, mind-reading, spiritualistic seances, crystal-gazing, and the like are taboo." But the reason Van Dine gives for this prohibition is that "The reader must have equal opportunity with the detective for solving the mystery. All clues must be plainly stated and described." It could be argued that certain of Hammett's stories are flawed in this sense. The plain fact is that this is not a primary value for Hammett, who is not out to construct the parlor game or mind puzzle of the Agatha Christie-Erle Stanley Gardner type.

To be fair, Van Dine's Twenty Rules—like his Philo Vance stories—are written in a spirit of fun. "Crimes by housebreakers and bandits are the province of the police departments—not of authors and brilliant amateur detectives," he writes in his explication of Rule No. 17. "A really fascinating crime is one committed by a pillar of a church, or a spinster noted for her charities." And if the process gets a little thin at times, it knows it is. But that in a way is also the point. A very different spirit guides Hammett's work—a new seriousness about the whole business of crime and criminals.

"If we place these popular writers [such as Christie and

Gardner] low in the critical scale," writes Albert Borowitz in *A Gallery of Sinister Perspectives: Ten Crimes and a Scandal* (Kent State University Press, 1982), "it may be because they ask and answer the least interesting questions about crime." Hammett's books are really less whodunits, in the traditional sense, than novels about the experiences of private detectives and others caught up in the world of crime. The emphasis is on character and motivation. Uncovering the identity of the killer is always less important, finally, than the exploration of the underlying theme of trust, winning and losing, the nature of evil and its relationship to society, or the individual's sense of honor in a corrupt world.

For if Hammett brought to the genre flesh-and-blood villains right off the pages of the daily newspaper, his detectives were all-too-human heroes prey to the same temptations, weaknesses, lapses into gullibility and the occasional less-than-noble motives as the rest of us. Even the Op's physical appearance is calculated to run athwart the ideal. He is short and paunchy and not especially handsome—a conspicuous departure from the romantic ideal—a man who obviously begins at a disadvantage. But all of these variations from the ideal have the effect not of painting him as an eccentric à la Hercule Poirot but, quite deliberately on Hammett's part, of making the Op more of an average man.

Curiously, he shares with the supercilious Philo Vance a certain heightened form of speech. The Op rarely just lights a cigarette, he "sets fire to a Fatima." Indeed there is a touch of the smart aleck about both men. But nothing else about the Op—his manner (businesslike), his other interests or hobbies (he has none), his appearance (nondescript), his brand of cigarette (no meerschaum pipe, no perfume-scented Reggies)—sets him apart from the crowd. He even drives a plain black coupe—"a type of car whose tamely respectable appearance makes it the ideal one for city work." He is the quintessential working-class hero who lives for his job and puts all his pride into doing it well, no matter what the obstacle.

Hammett seems deliberately to place the Op again and again in the employ of a client he does not respect precisely to make the point that the Op will perform his job anyway. His real loyalty, says story after story, is to himself. But the Op is no Mike Hammer, merely looking out for "Number One," no mere soldier of fortune who thinks only of his own skin or his own gratification. Rather, his loyalty is to a higher principle—the spark of a fire that has gone out in the world, which he keeps alive in himself. Garry Wills sees a touching resemblance between Hammett the radical, upholding "a private kind of honor in a rotten world," and his fictional detectives who serve society "without respecting it."

It is interesting to note that none of Hammett's heroes, after *The Dain Curse*, has a client in the true sense at all; from Sam Spade on, they act primarily on their own behalf. The old idealism persists, though it appears to be almost nonexistent in Spade until that last painful scene; with Ned Beaumont it is attached to an unworthy object; and it is quite muted in Nick Charles, who covers it over with a genteel and rather lovable hedonism. But it is always there, if only in their tacit refusal to take certain courses of action, or to act dishonorably. Even Nick Charles, though he does not go on about it, is clearly committed to decency and fairness and shows compassion toward the battered Dorothy Wynant and tolerance toward her lying brother. We learn on his visit to a speakeasy that he is regarded as a man of integrity even among the criminal class. It seems to be important to Hammett to make this point.

In this respect, Raymond Chandler was Hammett's spiritual heir. By a most fitting coincidence, his first story appeared in *Black Mask* the same year Hammett completed his last novel. Like Hammett, Chandler set his stories in the moral desert of California, in his case Los Angeles. Both men are romantics, but of the post-World War I variety. Gone is the old romantic faith that murder will out. Nothing will out, Hammett and Chandler seem to say, unless somebody pretty special makes it happen—"a man," in Chandler's famous phrase, "of honor."

Paradoxically, while Chandler clearly regarded Hammett as his master and had extravagant praise for Hammett's hard-won style, he evidently saw him as a sort of naif who was simply "trying to make a living by writing something he had firsthand information about." Chandler doubted, he said, "that Hammett had any deliberate artistic aims whatever." The fact that Hammett told James Thurber that *The Maltese Falcon* had been influenced by Henry James's *The Wings of the Dove* would seem to belie this peculiar charge, as does Hammett's careful reworking of the serial versions of his novels in bringing them into their hardcover forms. True, Hammett's style is less flashy than Chandler's, which is much more self-consciously literary in its flourishes, more obviously artful (if genuinely gifted) in its use of metaphor. Hammett's style, by contrast, is much more straightforward: a spare, lean vehicle for a world view that was wary of illusions. Even the more casual prose of his last two novels, which lacks the tense urgency of Hammett's most powerful writing, is still crisp and clean and to the point; he was a writer who seemingly could not write badly.

And, finally, what has been demonstrated here with regard to his deeper thematic concerns and their close relationship to the very structuring of Hammett's plots and juxtapositions of characters ought to refute once and for all the suggestion that Hammett was some sort of untutored folk artist who had no idea of craftsmanship—let alone deeper purposes—in writing his stories and novels. Indeed it has been the intent of this book to show precisely that.

It is chastening to remember that Hammett's considerable reputation is based on only five books. And the extent of his influence on succeeding generations of writers is all the more remarkable when one considers that he is represented on the library shelves by fewer titles than virtually any other well-known writer of detective novels in this century. The simple reason for this slender output is that, unlike such prolific authors as Sayers, Christie, Erle Stanley Gardner, Rex Stout, Georges Simenon, Mickey Spillane, John D. MacDonald, Ross Macdonald, Eric Ambler, John Dickson Carr or Walter Gibson, creator of The Shadow, who turned out more than one hundred books in that popular series, Hammett approached each of his novels as a fresh problem in theme and form. Even the two Op books are, as we have seen, very different in spirit and in their underlying preoccupations.

Each of Hammett's novels, as it were, opened up a new path that was subsequently explored by other writers. The novels of Mickey Spillane, beginning with *I, the Jury* (1947), might be traced—as might the more sophisticated struggles of Travis McGee—back to the violence and cynicism of *Red Harvest*; Ross Macdonald's ritual uncovering of sordid family histories to *The Dain Curse*; Raymond Chandler's vulnerable loner Philip Marlowe to *The*

Maltese Falcon; and every breezy man-woman team from Edward Lockridge's Mr. and Mrs. North . . . to The Avengers, to *The Thin Man*. James Bond's blend of insouciance, cold expertise and an eye for the ladies brings no earlier figure so much to mind as Nick Charles.

Hammett's work was seminal, in a way that the work of others was not. He exploded the form he inherited and revealed the richness of its possibilities. Through the movies—and especially the radio shows—based on his books, he helped shape the character of those young media and their approach to cops-and-robbers material. Shows like Jack Webb's *Dragnet*—and even the new adult westerns like *Gunsmoke*—which later crossed over to television, reveal the influence of Hammett's innovations in character and dialogue. If a part of what Hammett did was to bring the American western into a twentieth-century urban setting, Matt Dillon is unthinkable without the Op.

So great has been his influence, and so many his imitators, that Hammett's own work has ironically lost some of its edge and probably a good deal of its impact for present-day readers. But the testimony of many a writer—from Chandler to Ross Macdonald—has reaffirmed the freshness and originality, the command of his craft, the sheer *authority* that still stands in the five novels of Samuel Dashiell Hammett and the best of his stories. After more than fifty years, they are still the standard against which all comers know they must measure their own achievements.

Notes

References are identified by page number and the last three words of each quotation. Notes to Hammett's works are included only where the reference cannot be readily determined from the text. All references to Hammett's fiction are to the paperback editions. Date and publisher are given here only for sources that do not appear in the Bibliography.

Chapter 1

Page	Quote	Source
1	myself a businessman	R. J. Unstead, *The Twenties: An Illustrated History in Colour, 1919—1929*, p. 13.
1	stopped to rest	Lillian Hellman, *An Unfinished Woman*, p. 263.
1	the organization's office	Ibid., p. 261.
2	keeping my word	Ibid., p. 262.
2	Communism worried him	Ibid., p. 264.
2	his own terms	Hellman, *An Unfinished Woman*, p. 277.
2	"happy" in the army	Ibid., p. 274.
2	cell-block lavatories	Ibid., p. 263.
2	a rotten world	Garry Wills, Introduction to *Scoundrel Time* by Lillian Hellman, p. 32.
2	him as "sir"	Hellman, *An Unfinished Woman*, p. 271.
2	and pitiable frauds	Ibid., pp. 64–65.
2	wanted it more	Ibid., p. 269.

2	sick man sicker	Ibid., p. 263.
3	complicated by cancer	Ibid., p. 257.
3	and Patuxent Rivers	The facts of Hammett's biography are taken from a letter he wrote to *Black Mask,* November 1924, and various biographies (See Bibliography).
3	of the ceremony	Hellman, *Scoundrel Time,* p. 127.
3	A passionate Marxist	Hellman, *An Unfinished Woman,* p. 264.
3	up his world	Lillian Hellman, *Pentimento,* p. 173.
3	him to stay	Hellman, *An Unfinished Woman,* p. 271.
4	be very interesting	H. L. Mencken, *The American Language,* 3 vols (New York: Alfred A. Knopf, 1962). Fourth edition. Passim.
4	be very interesting	Hammett, "From the Memoirs of a Private Detective," *Smart Set,* March 1923; reprinted in Haycraft, *The Art of the Mystery Story,* pp. 418–420.
4	his voracious reading	Hellman, *An Unfinished Woman,* p. 273.
4	scars from knife	Ibid., p. 260.
5	His Pinkerton blackjack	William F. Nolan, *Dashiell Hammett: A Casebook,* p. 16.
6	backed the rattlers	Ibid., p. 17.
6	An incident involving	Hellman, *An Unfinished Woman,* p. 266.
7	don't like it	Hellman, *Pentimento,* p. 98.
7	Hammett confided to	Hellman, *Scoundrel Time,* pp. 47–48.
7	or no good	Hellman, *An Unfinished Woman,* p. 179.
7	had become intolerable	Hellman, *Scoundrel Time,* p. 48.
7	would not live	Hellman, *An Unfinished Woman,*
8	". . . and His Wife"	Included in the Hammett collection, *A Man Named Thin* (Joseph W. Ferman, 1962).

8	sensational "pulp" fiction	Facts in this and in the following paragraph are taken from Tony Goodstone's introduction to *The Pulps: Fifty Years of American Popular Culture*.
9	Fu Manchu	Sax Rohmer's popular Oriental villain, featured in a series of novels begun in 1913. See William F. Wu, *The Yellow Peril*, chapter 6.
9	least twenty years	Goodstone, *The Pulps*, p. xiii.
9	the branch again?	Earl Derr Biggers, "Keeper of the Keys," *The Saturday Evening Post*, June 11, 1932.
9	a spinsterish tearoom	Raymond Chandler, "The Simple Art of Murder," *The Atlantic Monthly*, December 1944; reprinted in a revised version in *The Saturday Review of Literature*, April 15, 1950, p. 13.
10	revolution in lifestyle	Frederick Lewis Allen, *Only Yesterday: An Informal History of the Nineteen Twenties*, p. 7.
10	The black sedan	Ibid., p. 263.
11	among their neighbors	Ibid., p. 100.
11	the old dispensation	Unstead, *The Twenties*, pp. 6–7. See also Allen, *Only Yesterday*, pp. 88–107.
12	and clean living	Martha Saxton in *The Twenties*, ed. Jeffrey Weiss, p. 11.
12	one four-year period	Unstead, *The Twenties*, p. 42.
12	it's hospitality	Ibid., p. 13.
13	four hundred murders	Ibid., p. 43.
13	simply, "From Al."	Allen, *Only Yesterday*, p. 262.
13	Carroll John Daly	Daly's story, "Knights of the Open Palm," starring a private eye named Race Williams, was published in *Black Mask*, June 1, 1923. See William F. Nolan, "Carroll John Daly: The Forgotten Pioneer of the Private Eye," *The Armchair Detective*, October 1970, pp. 1–4.

13	hero ever created	Goodstone, *The Pulps,* p. x.
14	the "embarrassing" name	Edmund Wilson, "Who Cares Who Killed Roger Ackroyd?" *The New Yorker,* January 20, 1945; reprinted in *The Art of the Mystery Story,* ed. Howard Haycraft, p. 392.
14	American police history	S. S. Van Dine [pseud. of Willard Huntington Wright], Introduction to *The "Canary" Murder* Case in *A Philo Vance Weekend* (New York: Charles Scribner's Sons, 1927), p. v.
14	as a snob	Van Dine, *The Benson Murder Case* (New York: Charles Scribner's Sons, 1926), p. 9.
14	and instructive monograph	Ibid., pp. 6–7.
15	a similar impression	Ibid., p. 10.
15	refinement and gentility	Hammett, "The Big Knockover," in the Hammett collection, *The Big Knockover,* p. 399.
15	the same address	Nolan, *Dashiell Hammett: A Casebook,* p. 26.
15	in a letter	Ibid., p. 26.
15	several of him	Hammett's letter, "From the Author of 'Arson Plus,'" *Black Mask,* October 10, 1923, p. 127.
16	Indeed, he maintained	Richard Layman, *Shadow Man: The Life of Dashiell Hammett,* p. 46.
16	three-hundredth page	Hammett, review of *The Benson Murder Case* by S. S. Van Dine, *The Saturday Review of Literature,* January 15, 1927; reprinted in Haycraft, *The Art of The Mystery Story,* pp. 382–383.
16	be nobody's son	Nolan, *Dashiell Hammett: A Casebook,* p. 23.
17	squibs and . . . poems	Hellman, *An Unfinished Woman,* p. 232.

Chapter 2

19	into a taxi	Hammett, "The Tenth Clew," in the Hammett collection, *The Continental Op*, p. 35.
22	forms of rioting	Hammett, "The Golden Horseshoe," in the Hammett collection, *The Continental Op*, p. 45.
24	Turk Street block	Hammett, "The House in Turk Street," in *The Continental Op*, p. 93.
27	a sinister Oriental	See William F. Wu, *The Yellow Peril: Chinese Americans in American Fiction, 1850—1940*, pp. 184–187, for a discussion of "The House in Turk Street."
28	of his sanity	Hammett, "The Girl with the Silver Eyes," in *The Continental Op*, p. 128.
29	from other detectives	Hammett, letter to *Black Mask*, quoted in Nolan, *Dashiell Hammett: A Casebook*, p. 32.

Chapter 3

33	to the rug	Hammett, "The Gutting of Couffignal," in *The Big Knockover*, p. 36.
34	fear of consequences	Hammett, "The Whosis Kid," in *The Continental Op*, p. 182.
39	I trust you	Hammett, "The Main Death," in *The Continental Op*, p. 262.
41	*Sun Also Rises*	The first of Hemingway's novels, published a few months earlier, in 1926.
41	bloodiest to date	Ernest Hemingway, *Death in the Afternoon* (New York: Charles Scribner's Sons, 1932), p. 228. Hammett, on the other hand, did not admire Hemingway—at least after meeting him in person, as is evidenced in an explosive confronta-

tion recounted by Lillian Hellman in *An Unfinished Woman*, pp. 59–60.

42   best in Hemingway   André Gide, "An Imaginary Interview," trans. Malcolm Cowley, *The New Republic*, February 7, 1944, p. 186. Hammett, according to Richard Layman (*Shadow Man*, p. 164), did not appreciate Gide's adulation.

42   "Death and Company"   Hammett's last Op tale, which first appeared in *Black Mask* in November 1931, was reprinted in *Best American Mystery Stories of the Year*, Vol. 2, 1932. (It was also his last *Black Mask* story.)

42   require the best   Hammett, "The Farewell Murder," in *The Continental Op*, p. 284.

Chapter 4

45   anything personal concerned   Ibid., p. 282.

46   in his way   Hammett, "The Gatewood Caper," in *The Big Knockover*, p. 173.

48   sum of money   Hammett, "The Gutting of Couffignal," in *The Big Knockover*, p. 34.

48   discharge her housekeeper   Hammett, "From the Memoirs of a Private Detective."

51   it was raining   Hammett, "Fly Paper," in *The Big Knockover*, p. 50.

51   on any subject   Hammett, "The Scorched Face," in *The Big Knockover*, p. 91.

52   on suicidal jobs   Hammett, "The Big Knockover," in *The Big Knockover*, p. 359.

52   of infinite cruelty   Chandler, "The Simple Art of Murder."

54   Siegel and Shuster   See Dennis Dooley, "The Man of Tomorrow and the Boys of Yesterday," *Cleveland Magazine*, June 1973, pp. 53–58.

54   The Scarlet Pimpernel   The hero of a series of popular novels by Baroness Orczy, begun in 1905, recounting the fictional ex-

ploits of a daring young Englishman named Sir Percy Blakeny during the French Reign of Terror.

55	of the credible	Anonymous obituary in *The New York Times,* January 11, 1961, p. 47, which reads in part: "His prose was clean and entirely unique. His characters were as sharply defined as any in American fiction. His stories were as consistent as mathematics and as intricate as psychology."
55	best in America	Hammett, "This King Business," in *The Big Knockover,* pp. 117–118.

Chapter 5

59	women are dark	Hammett, "The Whosis Kid," in *The Continental Op,* pp. 209–210.
60	mannish gray clothes	Hammett, "Dead Yellow Women," in *The Big Knockover,* p. 191.
60	a Manchu	One of the Manchurian conquerors of China in 1644 whose own dynasty was subsequently overthrown by the 1911 revolution. See also Wu, *The Yellow Peril,* especially p. 186 et seq., for a discussion of "Dead Yellow Women."
62	the Arizona desert	Hammett, "Corkscrew," in *The Big Knockover,* p. 250.
63	Sheriff Bill Eldon	See Dorothy Hughes, *Erle Stanley Gardner: The Case of the Real Perry Mason* (New York: William Morrow & Company, 1978), p. 85.
63	". . . Killed Dan Odams"	Hammett's tale of revenge in the Montana Hills, which first appeared in *Black Mask,* January 15, 1924), was reprinted in *The Creeping Siamese* (Lawrence E. Spivak, 1950). (See Peter Wolfe, *Beams Falling: The Art of Dashiell Hammett,* p. 9, for a discussion.) Another western tale by Hammett, "Nightmare

Town," appeared in *Argosy All-Story Weekly,* December 1924.

63   the mythic figure

In *Love and Death in the American Novel* (New York: Stein and Day, 1975), p. 499, Leslie Fiedler calls "the private eye . . . the cowboy adapted to life on the city streets." See also Paul Skenazy, *The New Wild West: The Urban Mysteries of Dashiell Hammett and Raymond Chandler.*

64   Leatherstocking novels

An immensely popular series of books by James Fenimore Cooper set in the American wilderness that includes *The Pioneers* (1823), *The Last of the Mohicans* (1826), *The Prairie* (1827), in which the white hunter Bumppo dies, and *The Pathfinder* (1840) and *The Deerslayer* (1841), which recount other earlier adventures of Bumppo and his faithful Indian friend—who foreshadow the Lone Ranger and Tonto.

65   man for woman

Leslie Fiedler, "Come Back to the Raft Ag'in, Huck Honey," in *An End to Innocence: Essays on Culture and Politics* (New York: Stein and Day, 1972), p. 142.

66   on a side

Dooley, "The Sweet and the Cruel," *Cleveland Magazine,* November 1973, p. 70.

66   1925 "beer" wars

Stuart Berg Flexner, *I Hear America Talking: An Illustrated Treasury of American Words and Phrases* (New York: Van Nostrand Reinhold Company, 1976), p. 73.

66   likely to occur

Quoted in Nolan, *Dashiell Hammett: A Casebook,* p. 43.

68   Angel Grace Cardigan

Grace made her debut in Hammett's story, "The Second-Story Angel,"

		Black Mask, November 15, 1923, later reprinted in the 1962 Hammett collection, *A Man Named Thin.*
69	nodded, smiling benignantly	Hammett, "$106,000 Blood Money," *Black Mask,* May 1927; reprinted in *The Big Knockover,* p. 458.
69	his former energy	John Updike, "Bech Meets Me," *Picked-Up Pieces* (New York: Alfred A. Knopf, 1975), p. 13.

Chapter 6

73	and savage place	Dante Alighieri, *The Divine Comedy,* trans. Lawrence Grant White (New York: Pantheon Books, 1948), p. 1.
74	artistic aims whatever	Chandler, "The Simple Art of Murder."
77	in the 1920's	See Allen, *Only Yesterday,* Chapter 3, "The Big Red Scare."
77	violent mass action	Ibid., p. 47.
77	the old sense	Ibid., pp. 61–62.
77	example of them	Ibid., pp. 84–86.
81	about his "soul"	For the original passage, see "The Big Knockover," in *The Big Knockover,* p. 368. The revised version appears on pp. 108–109 of *Red Harvest.*
83	in existing societies	John G. Cawelti, *Adventure, Mystery, and Romance: Formula Stories as Art and Popular Culture,* p. 173.
84	come to this	Dante Alighieri, *The Inferno,* trans. John Ciardi (New Brunswick, N.J.: Rutgers University Press, 1954), p. 72.
84	Hammett utilized Poisonville	Nolan, *Dashiell Hammett: A Casebook,* p. 47.

Chapter 7

87	of one mind	Hammett, *The Dain Curse*, p. 155.
90	Fitzstephan closely parallels	Nolan, *Dashiell Hammett: A Casebook*, p. 54.
93	expanded its role	Ibid., p. 54.
96	have heavily reworked	Ibid., p. 54.
97	increased . . . by 30,000	Ibid., p. 55.
98	has yet produced	Dust jacket blurb for *The Glass Key* (New York: Alfred A. Knopf, 1931).

Chapter 8

99	and do it	Hammett, *The Maltese Falcon*, p. 227.
104	you explain it	Stephen A. Leacock, "The Great Detective," reprinted in the Leacock collection, *Laugh With Leacock* (New York: Dodd, Mead & Company, 1946; orig. pub. 1930), p. 29.
104	little-did-he-realize	Hammett, review of S. S. Van Dine's *The Benson Murder Case,* in Haycraft, *The Art of the Mystery Story,* p. 383.
108	are made of	The complete screenplay is found in John Huston's *The Maltese Falcon,* ed. Richard J. Anobile (New York: The Film Classics Library, Universe Books, 1974). More than 1,400 frame blowup photos accompany the dialogue.
108	twenty-eight books	A full list appears in Nolan, *Dashiell Hammett: A Casebook,* pp. 149–151.
108	ignorant, as ever	Hammett, review of *The Scarab Murder Case, The New York Evening Post,* May 24, 1930.
109	Van Dine's Sixth Rule	S. S. Van Dine, "Twenty Rules for Writing Detective Stories," *American Magazine,* September 1928; re-

		printed in Haycraft, *The Art of the Mystery Story,* p. 190.
109	let it go	Hammett, *The Maltese Falcon,* p. 266.
112	snakes in dreams	"Among the less easily understandable male sexual symbols are certain *reptiles* and *fishes,* and above all the famous symbol of the *snake,"* states Sigmund Freud in *The Complete Introductory Lectures on Psychoanalysis,* Standard Edition, trans. and ed. by James Strachey (New York: W. W. Norton & Company, Inc., 1966). The quote is taken from Freud's 1916 lecture on dreams. According to Allen, *Only Yesterday,* pp. 98–99, Freud's theories were being widely discussed in America in the late 1920's.
113	never quite willing	Hellman, interview with Marilyn Berger, *Lillian Hellman: A Profile,* a five-part documentary series produced by KERA in Dallas and aired on PBS, April 1981.

Chapter 9

117	we believe happened	Gerald White Johnson, *American Heroes and Hero-Worship* (New York: Harper & Brothers, 1943), p. 5.
117	Long before *The*	Parts of this chapter appeared in a slightly different form in the Cleveland *Plain Dealer Friday Magazine,* December 14, 1979, p. 9.
118	Laurel and Hardy	Jon Tuska, *The Detective in Hollywood* (New York: Doubleday & Company, 1970), p. 180. Tuska attributes the *mot* to Peter Lorre.
118	had become "bored"	Hammett in a 1957 interview,

		quoted by Layman, *Shadow Man,* p. 147.
118	even for $40,000	Quoted by Tuska, *The Detective in Hollywood,* p. 201.
118	the first version	The aborted 1930 draft of *The Thin Man* was printed in the special Hammett issue of *City of San Francisco* magazine, ed. David Fechheimer, November 4, 1975.
119	and the villainess	Hellman, *An Unfinished Woman,* p. 270.
120	writer Ambrose Bierce	Oscar Levant, *The Unimportance of Being Oscar* (New York: G. P. Putnam's Sons, 1968), p. 179.
120	a "two-fisted loafer"	Quoted by Layman, *Shadow Man,* p. 146.
122	to Nick Charles	Ibid., pp. 141–142.
122	into a novel	Ibid., p. 144.
122	Hellman told friends	Layman, *Shadow Man,* p. 145.
124	fine time together	Hellman, *An Unfinished Woman,* p. 270.
127	next eighteen years	Ibid., p. 258.
127	quintessential "job-holder"	David T. Bazelon, "Dashiell Hammett's Private Eye," in *Nothing But a Fine Tooth Comb: Essays in Social Criticism, 1944–1969,* p. 250.
128	who was I	Malcolm Cowley, "Looking for the Essential Me," *The New York Times Book Review,* June 17, 1984, p. 18.
131	nearly one million	Layman, *Shadow Man,* p. 141.
131	*Secret Agent X-9*	According to Geoffrey O'Brien (*Village Voice,* July 12, 1983), Hammett only wrote for the comic strip for about a year. The strips he collaborated on have been reprinted in *Secret Agent X-9* by International Polygonics, Ltd. ($9.95 paper).

Chapter 10

| 133 | a botched civilization | Ezra Pound, "Hugh Selwyn Mauberley," in *Personae: The Col-* |

lected Shorter Poems of Ezra
Pound (New York: New Directions,
1971), p. 191.

133	to feel ashamed	*Lilliam Hellman: A Profile.*
134	much to me	Hammett, "Tulip," in *The Big Knockover,* p. 336.
135	broken his health	Hellman, *An Unfinished Woman,* p. 256.
136	C. Auguste Dupin	Bruce Cassiday, ed., *Roots of Detection* (New York: Ungar, 1983), p. 95. Includes an excerpt from the *Memoirs* of Vidocq.
137	test of time	See Dennis Dooley, "The Venerable Charlie Chan," *The Plain Dealer Magazine,* December 16, 1979.
137	c'est une faute	Van Dine, *The Benson Murder Case,* p. 9. Fouché (1763-1820) was Napoleon's Minister of Police.
138	two presidents confessed	Tuska, *The Detective in Hollywood,* pp. 25–26.
138	actor William Powell	Ibid., p. 28. Basil Rathbone portrayed Vance for MGM in *The Bishop Murder Case* (1930).
138	on a page	Edmund Wilson, "Who Cares Who Killed Roger Ackroyd?" in Haycraft's *The Art of the Mystery Story,* p. 393.
139	in his hand	Chandler, "The Simple Art of Murder," reprinted in a revised version in the Chandler collection, *The Simple Art of Murder* (New York: Houghton Mifflin Company, 1950), pp. vii–ix.
139	in public places	Ezra Pound, "Hugh Selwyn Mauberley," in *Personae,* p. 190.
140	of certain certainties	T. S. Eliot, "Preludes," in *The Complete Poems and Plays, 1909–1950* (New York: Harcourt, Brace & World, Inc., 1952), p. 13.
140	went its rounds	Allen, *Only Yesterday,* p. 122.
140	Mah Jong table	Ibid., p. 99.
143	rudimentary police routine	Hammett, review of *The Benson*

		Murder Case, in Haycraft, *The Art of the Mystery Story,* p. 382.
143	Twenty Rules for	Ibid., pp. 189–193.
144	spirit of fun	Haycraft also reprints, among other delightful manifestos, Ronald A. Knox's "A Detective Story Decalogue," which prescribes that "Not more than one secret room or passage is allowable" (Rule 3), that "No Chinaman must figure in the story" (Rule 5) and that "The stupid friend of the detective, the Watson, must not conceal any thoughts which pass through his mind; his intelligence must be slightly, but very slightly, below that of the average reader" (Rule 10).
145	questions about crime	Albert Borowitz, *A Gallery of Sinister Perspectives,* p. 1.
145	for city work	Hammett, "The Whosis Kid," in *The Continental Op,* p. 185.
146	without respecting it	Wills, Introduction to *Scoundrel Time* by Lillian Hellman, p. 33.
146	man . . . of honor	Chandler, "The Simple Art of Murder."
146	artistic aims whatever	Ibid.
146	told James Thurber	James Thurber, *Lanterns and Lances* (New York: Time Incorporated Book Division, 1955), p. 77. "In both novels," notes Thurber, "a fabulous fortune—jewels in *The Falcon,* inherited millions in *The Dove*—shapes the destinies of the disenchanted central characters; James's designing woman Kate Croy, like Hammett's pistol-packing babe Brigid O'Shaughnessy, loses her lover, although James's Renunciation Scene is managed, as who should say, rather more exquisitely than Hammett's. . . ."

147	of The Shadow	According to *The Great Detectives: A Host of the World's Most Celebrated Sleuths Are Unmasked by Their Authors,* ed. Otto Penzler (Boston & Toronto: Little, Brown & Company, 1978), *The Shadow* ran for 325 numbers 282 of which were written by Gibson (p. 206).
147	by other writers	Similarities have also been noted between *Red Harvest* and John D. MacDonald's *The Green Ripper* (1979) and Horace McCoy's *No Pockets in a Shroud.* Hammett's influence can also perhaps be seen in Graham Greene's *This Gun for Hire,* Frederick Forsyth's *The Day of the Jackal* and the novels of George V. Higgins.
148	and Mrs. North	This famous team of married sleuths, featured in several novels and a television show, began as characters in a 1936 series of sketches that appeared in *The New Yorker.*

Bibliography

I. Works by Hammett

A. *Novels*

Red Harvest. New York: Alfred A. Knopf, 1929. (Vintage Books Edition, October 1972.) Dedication is to Joseph Thomas Shaw, editor of *Black Mask.*

The Dain Curse. New York: Alfred A. Knopf, 1929. (Vintage Books Edition, October 1972.) Dedication is to Albert S. Samuels, the San Francisco jeweler for whom Hammett had worked for a time.

The Maltese Falcon. New York: Alfred A. Knopf, 1930. (Vintage Books Edition, May 1972.) Dedication is to Jose, Hammett's wife.

The Glass Key. New York: Alfred A. Knopf, 1931. (Vintage Books Edition, May 1972.) Dedication is to Nell Martin, a widowed piano player and music teacher with whom Hammett went off to New York (as Ned Beaumont and Janet Henry do at the end of the novel), after leaving his wife. Said to have been Hammett's own favorite among all his books.

The Thin Man. New York: Alfred A. Knopf, 1934. (Vintage Books Edition, May 1972.) Dedication is to Lillian.

B. *Short Fiction (in print)*

The Continental Op. New York: Vintage Books, 1975. With a literate introduction by Stephen Marcus. Includes "The Tenth Clew," "The Golden Horseshoe," "The House in Turk Street, "The Girl with the Silver Eyes," "The Whosis Kid," "The Main Death," and "The Farewell Murder."

The Big Knockover: Selected Stories and Short Novels by Dashiell Hammet. New York: Vintage Books, 1972. Edited and with an introduction

165

by Lillian Hellman, which was subsequently incorporated into her book-length memoir, *An Unfinished Woman*. Includes "The Gutting of Couffignal," "Fly Paper," "The Scorched Face," "This King Business," "The Gatewood Caper," "Dead Yellow Women," "Corkscrew," "Tulip," "The Big Knockover," and "$106,000 Blood Money."

C. *Other Writing by Hammett* (in print)

"From the Memoirs of a Private Detective," *Smart Set,* March 1923; reprinted in *The Art of the Mystery Story,* ed. Howard Haycraft, Simon and Schuster, Inc., 1946.

Review of *The Benson Murder Case, The Saturday Review of Literature,* January 15, 1927; reprinted in *The Art of the Mystery Story.*

II. Selected Works About Hammett

A. *Biographical*

Cooper, James. "Lean Years for the Thin Man," *Washington Daily News,* March 11, 1957. A candid interview with Hammett.

Feichheimer, David, ed. Special Hammett issue of *City of San Francisco* Magazine, November 4, 1975. Includes interviews with Hammett's friends and relatives and the original (1930) version of *The Thin Man*.

Hellman, Lillian. *Lillian Hellman: A Profile.* A five-part television documentary series in which Hellman is interviewed by Marilyn Berger at Hardscrabble Farm in Westchester County, N.Y. Produced by KERA in Dallas (aired on PBS in April 1981). Hellman talks about her career as a playwright, her relationship with Hammett, his career and their political troubles.

Hellman, Lillian. *An Unfinished Woman.* Boston & Toronto: Little, Brown and Company, 1969.

Hellman, Lillian. *Pentimento.* Boston & Toronto: Little, Brown and Company, 1973.

Hellman, Lillian. *Scoundrel Time.* Boston & Toronto: Little, Brown and Company, 1976. Introduction by Garry Wills.

Johnson, Diane. *Dashiell Hammett: A Life.* New York: Random House, 1983.

Layman, Richard. *Shadow Man: The Life of Dashiell Hammett.* New York and London: Harcourt Brace Jovanovich, 1981. Includes a full transcript of Hammett's testimony before the United States Second District Court, July 9, 1951, New York City.

Nolan, William F. *Hammett: A Life at the Edge.* New York: Congdon and Weed, 1983.

B. *Critical*

Bazelon, David T. "Dashiell Hammett's Private Eye," a 1949 *Commentary* essay, reprinted in *Nothing But a Fine Tooth Comb: Essays in Social Criticism, 1944–1969.* New York: Simon and Schuster, 1969.

Blair, Walter. "Dashiell Hammett: Themes and Techniques," in *Essays on American Literature in Honor of Jay B. Hubbell,* edited by Clarence Gohdes. Duke University Press, 1967.

Cawelti, John G. *Adventure, Mystery, and Romance: Formula Stories as Art and Popular Culture.* Chicago and London: University of Chicago Press, 1976. See chapter on Hammett, Chandler, and Spillane.

Chandler, Raymond. "The Simple Art of Murder," *The Atlantic Monthly,* December 1944; reprinted in a revised and greatly expanded version in *The Saturday Review of Literature,* April 15, 1950, and in the Chandler collection, *The Simple Art of Murder.* New York: Houghton Mifflin Company, 1950.

Durham, Philip. *Down These Means Streets a Man Must Go.* Chapel Hill: University of North Carolina Press, 1963. Classic study of Chandler's work that makes several references to Hammett.

Gide, André. "An Imaginary Interview," trans. Malcolm Cowley, *The New Republic,* February 7, 1944.

Goulart, Ron, ed. *The Hardboiled Dicks.* Sherbourne Press, 1965. Introduction considers Hammett's place in the movement.

Gruber, Frank. *The Pulp Jungle.* Sherbourne Press, 1967.

Harmon, Jim. *The Great Radio Heroes.* New York: Doubleday and Company, 1967. Section on the Hammett radio series includes dialogue excerpts.

Haycraft, Howard, ed. *Murder for Pleasure.* Appleton-Century, 1941. A history of the whodunit.

Maugham, W. Somerset. "The Decline and Fall of the Detective Story," in *The Vagrant Mood* (New York: Doubleday and Company, 1953).

Nolan, William F. *Dashiel Hammett: A Casebook.* Santa Barbara: McNally and Loftin, 1969. Introduction by Philip Durham. Has an extensive historical bibliography of Hammett's work in various media.

Schickel, Richard. "Dirty Work," *Book Week,* August 28, 1966. Some perceptive thoughts on Hammett's Op and his work ethic.

Shaw, Joseph T., ed. *The Hard-Boiled Omnibus.* New York: Simon and Schuster, Inc., 1946. An anthology of *Black Mask* fiction with an introduction by editor Shaw that puts Hammett in historical perspective.

Skenazy, Paul. *The New Wild West: The Urban Mysteries of Dashiell Hammett and Raymond Chandler.* Boise State University, 1982.

Tuska, Jon. *The Detective in Hollywood.* New York: Doubleday, 1978. Excellent chapters on the films of *The Maltese Falcon* and *The Thin Man.*

Wolfe, Peter. *Beams Falling: The Art of Dashiell Hammett.* Bowling Green University Popular Press, 1980.

C. *Bibliographical*

Layman, Richard. *Dashiell Hammett: A Descriptive Bibliography.* Pittsburgh: University of Pennsylvania Press, 1979.

Mundell, E. H. *A List of the Original Appearances of Dashiell Hammett's Magazine Work.* Kent State University Press, 1968.

III. General Background

Allen, Frederick Lewis. *Only Yesterday: An Informal History of the Nineteen Twenties.* New York and London: Harper and Brothers, 1931.

American Heritage, August 1965. Special issue on The Twenties. Combines rare illustrations with astute essays by several authors.

Booth, Ernest. "The Language of the Underworld," *American Mercury,* May 1928. "Brevity, conciseness is the essence of thieves' jargon," notes Booth, a former convict. "To be able to convey a warning and the nature of the danger in a single word or phrase is the test."

Goodstone, Tony, ed. *The Pulps: Fifty Years of American Popular Culture.* New York: Chelsea House, 1970. Selections include the 1924 Hammett story, "One Hour," and many vivid full-color reproductions of pulp magazine covers.

Haycraft, Howard, ed. *The Art of the Mystery Story.* New York: Simon and Schuster, Inc., 1946. A highly entertaining and useful anthology which brings together more than fifty hard-to-find fugitive pieces by many well-known writers—from Hammett ("From the Memoirs of a Private Detective") and Chandler ("The Simply Art of Murder") to S. S. Van

Dine ("Twenty Rules for Writing Detective Stories") and Edmund Wilson ("Who Cares Who Killed Roger Ackroyd?")

Maurer, David. "The Argot of the Underworld," *American Speech,* December 1931, pp. 99–118. "Its chief characters are its machine-gun staccato, its hard timbre, its rather grim humor, its remarkable compactness."

Maurer, David. *The Big Con.* Indianapolis, 1940. "Professional crime is nothing more than a great variety of highly specialized trades," notes the author, "hence it is only natural that many of the same factors which operate among legitimate craftsmen should affect criminal speech." (pp. 270–271).

Mencken, H. L. *The American Language: An Inquiry into the Development of English in the United States,* 4th edition. 3 vols. New York: Alfred A. Knopf, 1962. Supplies meanings of many obscure words, along with insightful commentary.

Ruhm, Herbert, ed. *The Hard-boiled Detective: Stories from* Black Mask *Magazine (1920–1951).* New York: Random House, 1977. Includes Carroll John Daly's "The False Burton Combs," Chandler's "Goldfish" and Hammett's "The Road Home" (written under the pseudonym of Peter Collinson).

Unstead, R. J. *The Twenties: An Illustrated History in Colour, 1919–1929.* London: Macdonald and Company, 1973.

Weiss, Jeffrey, ed. *The Twenties.* Consolidated Music Publishers, 1976. Includes a literate, often illuminating text by Martha Saxton and lyrics of many popular songs of the decade.

Wu, William F. *The Yellow Peril: Chinese Americans in American Fiction 1850–1940.* Archeon Books, 1982.

Index

Allen, Frederick, Lewis, 10–11, 77, 140
Antagonist, 23, 27–32, 40, 50, 62, 144, 145
  in *The Dain Curse*, 91, 94, 96–97
  in "The Girl with the Silver Eyes," 28–32
Astor, Mary, 101, 102

Benson Murder Case, The (S. S. Van Dine), 14, 16
"Big Knockover, The" (story), 51–52, 66–69, 81
Big Knockover, The (collection), 15, 19, 46–49, 54–55, 65
Black Mask (periodical), xiii, 8, 9, 15, 16, 19, 27, 29, 33, 42, 47, 65–66, 77, 88, 109, 146
  circulation of, 97
  hard-boiled detective fiction published in, 13
  as training ground for writers, 19–20, 141
  western stories published by, 63
Blood Money, 65, 73–74, 91
Bogart, Humphrey, 101–02

Cawelti, John G., 83
Celebrated Criminal Cases of America (Duke), 122–23

Chandler, Raymond, 9–10, 52, 139, 146, 147
Characterization, 21–24, 40, 46
  of foreigners, 26, 27, 42, 48–49, 55, 59, 62, 102
  in "The Girl with the Silver Eyes," 27–29
  of the Old Man, 51–53, 71, 81
  physical features as revelation of, 20, 23, 26, 29, 40
  See also Antagonist; Charles, Nick; Continental Op; Detective hero; O'Shaughnessy, Brigid; Spade, Sam
Charles, Nick, 119, 125–26
  detachment of, 124–25
  indolence of, 120–21
  past life of, 127–29
Children's Hour, The (Hellman), 131
Christie, Agatha, 12, 14, 96, 137–38
Cody, Phil, 13
Continental Op, 16
  competence of, 34–36, 49–50
  complex character of, 20–21, 23–24, 49–51, 70, 80–82, 94–96
  cynicism of, 36, 40, 47, 52, 56, 67, 69–70, 80–81, 91
  detachment of, 32, 33–37, 51–52, 54–55

genesis of, 15–16
idealism of, 57, 94–95
integrity of, 25, 38–39, 50–51, 58
physical appearance of, 31, 69, 145
as realistic detective hero, 15–17, 21–22
and Sam Spade, contrasted, 99–100
values of, 43–44
and Philo Vance, contrasted, 15–16
vulnerability of, xvii, 21–22, 26, 31, 35–36, 42–43, 50–51
and wealthy people, contempt for, 45–47, 54–55
Continental Op, The (collection), 19–32
"Corkscrew," 54, 62–65, 75–76
Cowley, Malcolm, 128
"Crooked Souls." *See* "Gatewood Caper, The"

Dain Curse, The, 41, 65, 88–98
Daly, Carroll John, 13
Dashiell Hammett: A Casebook (Nolan), 5
"Dead Yellow Women," 27, 54, 60–61, 143
"Death and Company," 42
Death in the Afternoon (Hemingway), 41
Detective hero, xii, xv, 15, 21–22, 31, 112, 145–46
and western hero, compared, 63
Detective story
Hammett's impact on, xii, xiv, 13, 135–36, 138–48
history of, xii, 135–36
Dialogue, 47, 53, 102
Doyle, Arthur Conan, 12, 54, 87, 136, 137

"Farewell Murder, The," 42–44, 45–51
Farewell to Arms, A (Hemingway), 5
Faulkner, William, 7, 119
Female characters. *See* Women characters
Fiedler, Leslie, 65
Fitzgerald, F. Scott, 5, 11, 12
Fleming, Ian, 148
"Fly Paper," 53–54, 73
"From the Memoirs of a Private Detective" (magazine article), 4, 65, 124, 143

Gallery of Sinister Perspectives, A (Borowitz), 145
Gardner, Erle Stanely, 9, 63
"Gatewood Capter, The," 17, 46–48
"Girl with the Silver Eyes, The," 27–32
characterization in, 27–28
ending of, 30–32, 34
violence in, sense of, 37–38
Glass Key, The, 109–15
integrity in, 112
motion picture versions of, 115
point of view in, 113
structure of, 114
theme of, 112–13
violence in, scenes of, 114
"Golden Horseshoe, The," 22–24
Goodstone, Tony, 9
"Great Detective, The" (Leacock), 104
Great Gatsby, The (Fitzgerald), 11
Greenstreet, Sydney, 101, 118
"Gutting of Couffignal, The," 48–49, 81

Hammett, Dashiell
as detective for Pinkerton Agency, 3–4, 5–7, 15–16

and detective story, impact on, xii, xiv, 13, 135–36, 138–48
health of, 2, 3, 5–7, 57–58, 126–27
imprisonment of, 1, 2
influences on fiction of, 139–41
as non-mystery writer, 7–8, 16–17, 63, 74, 108, 114, 119–20, 155–56n.
pseudonyms of, 16–17
values of, xiv, xv, 1–2, 6
Hammett, Josephine Dolan, 6, 113
Hammett, Mary Jane, 6
Hellman, Lillian, 1–3, 7, 118, 127, 131, 133
as anthologist of Hammett's works, 65
and Hammett, 113
as inspiration for Nora Charles, 119, 125
on *The Thin Man,* 122, 124
Hemingway, Ernest, 5, 94, 153n.
and Hammett, compared, 22, 41–42
"House in Turk Street, The," 24–27

Idealism, xvi
in Continental Op stories, 44, 57
Imagery. *See* Poker imagery; Religious imagery
In Our Time (Hemingway), 41
Integrity, 1–2, 112
of Continental Op, 25, 40, 50–51, 58
in *The Glass Key,* 112
Irony, 4, 27–28, 46, 48, 49, 69, 78

Layman, Richard, 122
Leacock, Stephen A., 104
Levant, Oscar, 119–20
Lorre, Peter, 101–02, 118
Loy, Myrna, 118

"Main Death, The," 39–42
Maltese Falcon, The, 98–108
foreshadowed in earlier works, 30, 51
motion picture versions of, 101, 108, 114, 117–18
point of view in, 104–07
theme of, 112–13
violence in, lack of, 114, 122
See also O'Shaughnessy, Brigid; Spade, Sam
"Man Who Killed Dan Odams, The," 63
Marcus, Steven, 20
Martin, Nell, 113
McCarthyism, xiii, 1–2
Men characters, friendships between, 64–65, 109–10
Metaphor, 75, 93, 123
Morality. *See* Values
Mysterious Affair at Styles, The (Christie), 14

1920, as background for Hammett's works, xiv, 10–13, 53, 65
Nolan, William F., 5, 84, 90, 97

"$106,000 Blood Money," 68, 69–71
O'Shaughnessy, Brigid, 105–07, 112
prefigured in earlier works, 30, 51

Pinkerton Detective Agency, 3–7, 16, 76
as background for Hammett's works, 29, 48, 93, 101, 141–42
Poe, Edgar Allan, 135–37
Poker imagery, 23, 39, 44, 71
in "The Gatewood Caper," 47
in *The Glass Key,* 111
in *The Maltese Falcon,* 107
in "This King Business," 56
in "The Whosis Kid," 36

Point of view
  in Continental Op stories, 16, 103,
    104
  in *The Glass Key*, 113
  in *The Maltese Falcon*, 103
  in Nero Wolfe stories (Stout), 104
  in *The Thin Man*, 118–19
  in traditional detective novel,
    103–04
Powell, William, 118, 138
Pseudonyms of Hammett, 16–17
Pulp fiction, 8–10, 13

Realism, 16, 31, 37–38, 83, 93, 143
  See also under Continental Op;
    Thin Man, The
Reality and appearance, 51, 94
Red Harvest, 65, 75–85, 126
  genesis of, 7
  motion picture based on, 114
  socialism in, 76–77
Religious imagery, 67–68, 81

Sanctuary (Faulkner), 7
Sayers, Dorothy, 12, 137
"Scorched Face, The," 51–53
Secret Agent X-9 (comic strip), 131,
  160n.
Settings, 54–55, 60–65
Shaw, Joseph T., 13, 66
"Simple Art of Murder, The"
  (Chandler), 9, 139
"Slippery Fingers," 17
Spade, Sam, xv, 99–101, 112–13
  and the Continental Op, con-
    trasted, 99–100
  genesis of, 15
  name of, 100, 107
Stout, Rex, 104
Style, 8, 19–27, 61–62, 147
  See also Imagery; Metaphor;
    Symbolism
Sutton, George W., Jr., 13, 15

Symbolism, 40, 112

"Tenth Clew, The," 20–22
Theme, 19–20, 88, 111–12, 127–29,
  145
  belief, exploitation of, 92–93, 95,
    96–97, 130–31
  commitment, 112–13
  reality and appearance, 21, 27, 28
  trust, 38–40, 105–06
  wealth and corruption, 45–48, 52–
    56, 60, 70, 78, 110
  women as exploiters of men's
    trust, 21, 65
Thin Man, The, 12, 117–34, 142, 143
  characters in, inspiration for,
    119–20, 134
  flaws in, 122–23, 124
  motion pictures based on, 115,
    117, 123
  violence in, lack of, 121–22
"This King Business," 54–57
Thurber, James, 146, 162n.

Values, 19–20, 43–46, 50–51
  See also Integrity
Van Dine, S. S., 14–16, 108–09, 137–
  38, 143–44
Villain. *See* Antagonist
Violence, scenes of, 9–10, 37–38,
  66, 70–74, 141

"Whosis Kid, The," 33–39
Wills, Garry, 2, 146
Wilson, Edmund, 14, 138
Women characters, 59, 60–61, 64, 94
  as exploiters of men's trust, 26,
    38–39, 65
  in *Red Harvest*, 79–81, 82
  in "This King Business," 59–60
Woollcott, Alexander, 98
Wright, Willard Huntington. *See*
  Van Dine, S. S.